"Without question, Craig Peters' book, *Navigating Toward Home*, is one of the most practical, down-to-earth books for men I have read in years. It is a passionate and powerful book on purpose-driven living in today's world. Craig writes with clarity and practicality and is in touch with issues that really trouble men everywhere. The wisdom put on the pages here, and the thoughtful suggestions and challenges are what make this book so powerful. *Navigating Toward Home* will continue to minister to your life each time you open it. I recommend it without reservation and will encourage every man I know who seriously wants to make a difference for God to read it and incorporate it thoroughly into his life. This should be required reading for every man!"

—Dr. Tom Thompson
Pastor of Assimilation and Small Groups
Shadow Mountain Community Church, California

"Chart your course for life with this biblically sound tool that will be an incredible encouragement to all the men who desire to fulfill God's plan for their life. Craig Peters writes practical and biblically based guidelines that prove to be a great resource aiding fathers as they navigate through their daily lives."

—Dr. Gary Rosberg
President, America's Family Coaches
Author of *Guard Your Heart* and *The Five Love Needs of Men and Women*

"My husband started reading *Navigating Toward Home*. I practically had to beg him to read it. One night he sat down and started reading it (because there wasn't anything good on T.V.). When I went to bed at 10:30, he was still reading it. As I went to go upstairs, he thanked me and said, "There's some great stuff in here." I wept with joy as I walked into the bedroom. Little did I know, but that night God began to navigate my husband back to me and my children. Thank you, Craig, for writing such a timely book for my husband and many others."

—A rejoicing spouse

D1503337

"Craig's use of humor and wit creates the perfect atmosphere, allowing men to be comfortable while seriously addressing issues of faith. I especially appreciate the candor he brings to the discussion of barriers that challenge men in relationships."

—Mark Lile, Pastor
Hudson Community Chapel, Ohio

"Craig speaks with great enthusiasm and with a great passion for men's ministry. His message reflects a heart for men, as well as a transparency about his own struggles as a man."

—Dr. Byron Morgan, Pastor
Mountain View Church, Marietta, Georgia

"*Navigating Toward Home* is fresh and new. It's easy to read, faithful to the text—the Bible—and very personal. It's realistic. Craig treats life like it is—often hard. I think the book would especially be good with small groups... Thanks to Craig Peters for writing in such a creative way."

—Pastor Knute Larson
The Chapel, Akron, Ohio

Navigating Toward Home

Navigating Toward Home

Charting Your Course
Toward Biblical Manhood

CRAIG PETERS

Evergreen
PRESS

Navigating Toward Home
by Craig Peters
Copyright ©2000 Craig Peters

ISBN 1-58169-047-9
For Worldwide Distribution
Printed in the U.S.A.

Evergreen Press
An Imprint of Genesis Communications, Inc.
P.O. Box 91011 • Mobile, AL 36691
800-367-8203
Email: EvergreenBooks@aol.com
website: ievergreenpress.com

TABLE OF CONTENTS

Coordinate # 6
NAVIGATING OUR MARRIAGE AND FAMILY

Coordinate # 7
NAVIGATING THROUGH THE STORMS OF LIFE

Coordinate # 8
NAVIGATING TOWARD VALUABLE FRIENDSHIPS

EPILOGUE

FOREWORD

I lose more friends this way!

Just because I blindly lucked out and got a big-selling book on the market, all of a sudden every pastor friend of mine figures I'm some great-shakes literary genius. And I'm constantly hearing, "Just take a quick look at this new book of mine, and lemme know what you think." Talk about the rock and the hard place–what are you going to tell them?

"Sorry, Tom, it stinks," you almost want to yell!

"Gee, Paul, I know you really love the Lord and all that, but–er–ah–man–I don't know how to tell you this–but forget that book!"

Even the "spiritual" route never seems to work, "Harry, do you really feel the Lord has led you to write this…thing?"

And I really shuddered when Craig Peters' manuscript arrived at my desk! Craig's probably my favorite pastor in the whole world. But, I've always figured him for a particularly sensitive and sweet brother, so how in the world am I going to tell him–of all pastors–that his book doesn't cut it?

But then I read it. And I mean I really read it–no skimming! And it is–by far–the most outstanding Christian nuts and bolts how to really get close to the Lord book I've ever read in over a quarter of a century in ministry! *Navigating Toward Home* ought to be required reading for every Christian in America!

Whether you're a believer or not, it's everything you ever wanted to know about what's missing in your life, and how to find it!

Shoot! I'm gonna go back and re-read it again right now!

Because He lives!
Dr. Gene Neill, President World-Wide Prison Ministries

ACKNOWLEDGMENTS

It takes a devoted and sacrificial crew to get from point A to point B. This project would have become shipwrecked if it wasn't for the encouragement and prayers of so many who unselfishly came aboard. My sincerest gratitude for the many who saw the giftedness in me to relate to men on a level that would grip their heart for the glory of God and create Biblical change. Here's a salute to the many who kept me on course and made this journey so enjoyable.

• To my devoted and loving wife, Ann, and my three children: Amanda, Nicole, and Jared. You make coming home the highlight of my day. I'd stand at the helm in any storm for you. You encourage, inspire and make me laugh like no others.

• To Marlene Bagnull who was the first to read this "stuff" at a writers conference and believed in me enough to see that this book was different from others.

• To Dr. Gene Neill. Thanks for your wonderful friendship and example. Prisons have never been the same since you showed your face.

• To Brenda Cunningham who worked endless hours reading, editing and correcting my spelling errors. You make me look way too good. I am honored!

• To my agent and friend, Renee McKenney, who has spent more money on postage getting out my manuscript than anyone I know. Thank you for believing in me, and putting a thumb to my back.

• To the men at Maranatha Bible Church who kept asking when would I be done, so they could get a copy. I love you brothers and enjoy seeking God's face together. It's a privilege to be on board with such a faithful crew of godly men.

• To my friend and comrade, Jim Creed, who had the guts to walk out on the plank with me and encourage me to live my dreams. You really do pump me up!

• To the church body at Maranatha. May God equip you in your life so you may ride the wave of righteousness as you move closer to the Son of God. You make pastoring a delight!

• To the elders and staff at Maranatha: I appreciate the care, counsel and prayers.

• To my "Ranger Buddies" who have seen the good and not so good of me and still stick with me. I couldn't ask for more influential friends than you. Truly, "together is better than being alone!"

• To my Lord and Savior who has been my compass and light during times when I could not see the way. It's an honor to sail this journey with You.

• And to you, the reader: I've prayed for you. Long before you picked up this book, I asked that God would open your heart and navigate you to Himself. May God's coordinates lead you in the way everlasting. I'm honored that you would read these pages.

DEDICATION

To my parents:
Thank you for all your love and support
along the way.

Chapter 1
DRIFTING

*We must pay more careful attention, therefore, to what
we have heard, so that we do not drift away.*
—Hebrews 2:1

Leaning against a sign post, John stopped to examine the worn-out sole of his shoe. He had neglected to get it fixed for over a week now. The heavy rain, having fallen the night before, left hula hoop sized puddles on the sidewalk. There was no way he could dodge them without jumping into the morning rush hour traffic and getting picked off by a car. Half running, half hopping, John made his way down the sidewalk avoiding the biggest ones. Eventually his foot found just enough of a puddle to soak his socks and shoes. He winced at the squishing noise he made with every step.

Just another reminder, John thought, *of the worn-out and miserable life I've somehow stepped into this past year.* John compared his relationship with his wife to two ships that pass in the night—distant, silent, and cold. Communication with Jane was at an all-time low these days. He had seen their marriage drifting for quite a while, but had chosen to ignore it, hoping it would straighten itself out. Now he was reaping the consequences of his neglect.

Work was a zoo, and more hours were expected if the promotion he was hoping to get would come through. Getting up earlier and staying at work later wasn't helping either his short fused temperament or family harmony.

Drifting, John thought, *I'm just drifting. I can't remember the last time I took a day off. I can't recall the last time when our family laughed so hard it hurt, or shared an evening of playing games and eating popcorn. Or when Jane and I snuggled under a blanket watching the wood burn in our fireplace. Things were simpler before. Purpose and focus on what really mattered in life was so clear, so defined. I was right on course: romantic, energetic, passionate for my family and the Lord. But recently my vision has become blurred somewhere...*

As John switched his scuffed briefcase into his right hand to protect it from the sheets of water thrown up by the passing cars, he thought about how it probably had weathered the storms of life better than he had. Reports, day planner, memos, unanswered phone messages, and today's urgencies were stuffed into the briefcase—taken home last night, but never touched.

Exhausted and thoroughly soaked by the time he arrived at his office building, John crammed his way into the corporate elevator. When he finally reached his office, he threw his soggy coat and umbrella on a swivel chair and dragged himself behind his desk to begin another day.

"Good morning," Nancy, his secretary, greeted him.

What's so good about it? John thought.

"Congratulations on being with the company for 15 years!" she continued as she handed him a cup of coffee. "The Robinson project is on for today. You have an appointment at 8:00, one at 9:00, another at 11:00. You have lunch with the people on the Robinson project at 12:30, and Mr. Shackley would like you to clear your schedule for the afternoon."

Clear my schedule? John thought, as Nancy left. *I can't even clear my thoughts! How in the world did I ever end up here? I keep telling myself and my family that things are going to change—we'll get away, spend time together, become a family again. But lately my promises have fallen flat—the look in their faces tells me that they know it's not going to happen.*

Opening his briefcase, John's eyes focused on a discolored and worn-out photograph of his family that had been taken while on vacation years ago. It had fallen out from one of the pockets, landing right next to the Cross pen he had received last Friday at a party celebrating his 15th year of commitment to the company.

Picking it up, John thought, *I work 15 years, giving it my all and what happens? I get a pen! I'm married to my job. I've brought my family to the threshold of disaster. My friends have come and gone. My journey with Christ has become almost non-existent.*

Drifting. I've been slowly drifting away from what I know to be true. Somewhere I steered off course, and I've lost my way. I've sacrificed my life and those around me, for a pat on the back and a lousy pen. How did I ever end up here?

As he looked at the photograph, John wondered if he would ever be able to see smiles like those on the faces of his wife and children again. "It's time to go home," John said out loud.

"What was that, John?" Nancy replied. "Are you on the phone? Your 8:00 meeting will be here in 15 minutes. Are you all right?"

John glanced up from the picture. "I am now. I'm taking the day off."

"What?" said Nancy.

"Yeah, I'm taking the day off."

"Wh-what are you going to do with all your meetings? What about the Robinson project and meeting with Mr. Shackley?"

"Nancy," said John, "reschedule for another day. I love this company, but they can wait. There are others who can't wait any longer."

"Where are you going?"

John smiled, looking down at his worn out shoe and then at the photograph. "I guess you could say I'm going to get my 'soul' fixed."

John had lost his way. It hadn't happened overnight. It usually doesn't. Like John, many of us have looked up from life's voyage and realized we have somehow drifted off course. For some of us it takes months, even years, before we are awakened to the stark reality that we have entered into dangerously unfamiliar waters.

So we look for a sign, a flare, a point of reference, anything. But all that was familiar and meaningful at one time has somehow disappeared, leaving us wondering which way is home.

Questions and feelings of panic flood the soul.

I'm lost! How can I get back? Can I get back? Where do I turn? Are there reliable coordinates I can use in my life that will assure me I'm headed toward home?

3

Suddenly we're driven to find what had once been part of our familiar life and not let it out of our sight. We want to get it in full view, so that we don't stray too far off course.

Many of us have experienced that revelation and then felt a hollow pit in our stomach, because we know we've lost sight of what has lasting significance:

- The stability of an honorable marriage.
- The harmony of a happy home.
- The bonds of lasting relationships.
- The guidance of our heavenly Father.

Consider these questions that can grip our soul and help us in becoming once again a vessel of honor for the Master no matter what their condition or how far we have drifted from the Father:

1. Do you find yourself barely staying afloat due to the difficulties of life that never seem to cease?

2. Do you find yourself skimming through life, events, relationships, and priorities, giving a piece of yourself to everyone and everything, but rarely having time to enjoy life's journey?

3. Do you experience victories in your walk as a man of God on a daily, weekly, monthly basis? Or are you just kidding yourself?

4. Are you *under* the pile or staying *on top* of it?

5. Do you have an inner passion to be God's man and to consistently represent Him in your day-to-day living?

I think of myself as a pretty simple individual. I love the Lord, I want to make a difference for His Kingdom, and I want to create a legacy today worth leaving for my family and friends tomorrow. But life can be very difficult along the way. We need all the wisdom we can get. I enjoy advice that is short and to the point. No mincing words. Say what you mean and mean what you say, and then go on. That's why I love the Bible so much. Our Lord doesn't sugarcoat or dance around what needs to be said and done for us to maintain a correct course in righteous living. Nor does He try to dazzle or impress us with terms and phrases that cause us to think twice about trying to understand the Creator of heaven and earth. No, His coordinates are precise, accurate, and easy enough for a child to follow. Yet they are thought provoking enough for the professor of theology to marvel over. They're just what a person needs in navigating himself back on track from where he's drifted.

The intention of this book is to encourage and strengthen you to see that righteous living is attainable, but only through the biblical co-ordinates of God's Word. This must be our reference point throughout our journey in life. Without His coordinates saturating our soul, we are doomed like John to a miserable life. When we lose our focus we will surely drift off course, and getting back is never easy, convenient, or in-stantaneous. Therefore, we need God's help to see us through by pro-ducing within us proper habits, priorities, and godly character that will help us successfully navigate through life.

Somewhere, within our private thoughts, if we listen close enough, is a familiar voice of One calling in the night to turn our heart toward home. Like John, it's not too late to let our heavenly Father navigate our lives according to the reliable coordinates of His Word.

I hope these biblical coordinates will minister to you as you turn your heart toward the Father who loves you. The sun is rising—it's a new day. It's time to navigate toward home.

CHARTING YOUR COURSE

SELF-EVALUATION

1. Can you relate to where John is in this story? As you observe your life, where might you be drifting and in need of help to get back on course?

2. Take a piece of paper and write down:
   A. Areas where you are *"on course"* where your heart and mind are fixed on obeying the coordinates of the Word of God (see Proverbs 4:25-27; Hebrews 12:2-3).
   B. Areas in your life where you are *drifting slightly*, where God's coordinates are forgotten or ignored at times due to distractions.
   C. Areas where drifting has taken you into *unfamiliar territory* and is putting you and those who love you at risk; areas where God's

coordinates are disregarded and distractions are numerous, resulting in a damaged vessel to your faith, family, and friendships. (See 1 Timothy 1:19 in contrast with 2 Timothy 2:21.)

3. How do you respond when you realize that you have drifted off course and have lost your way?

GROUP DISCUSSION

1. Where, like John, do men tend to steer off course and lose their way?

2. What value do you place on the following? In what practical ways is that manifested in a man's life?
  • The stability of an honorable marriage.
  • The harmony of a happy home.
  • The bonds of lasting relationships.
  • The guidance of our heavenly Father.

3. What biblical characters can you identify who have at some point lost their way? In what ways did the drifting process begin? How did God eventually turn their hearts toward home?

4. Commit yourself anew to the Lord by praying or reading aloud Psalm 26.

Music Resource*

"Making My Way Back Home" by Benjamin, off the *Benjamin* CD, 1994, Ariose Music, a division of Star Song Communication.

Author's note: My heartfelt desire is for you to take advantage of the many resources throughout the book. These provide further insights for both individual and group study.

COORDINATE #1

Navigating
Toward
Biblical Identity

Chapter 2
WHO'S IN THE CROW'S NEST?

"For His eye is on the sparrow and I know He watches me."
(classic gospel song)

A man standing in the crow's nest—that's how it began. Frederick Fleet was perched halfway up the foremast peering out into the cold, dark night at 11:40 p.m., Sunday, April 14, 1912.

Fleet found the ocean unusually calm. As the Titanic forged its way through the waters at 22 knots, the stars burned bright on the moonless night. Fleet's breath was visible in the darkness. The contrast between the ocean and the sky made a vivid dark line on the horizon. Below the line lay a black Atlantic.

Suddenly, the sailor noticed something strange straight ahead, right on the horizon—an obstruction of some kind. First one, then two, then several appeared, as he squinted to see what was ahead. They continued to grow larger as they loomed closer with every ticking moment.

Oh, God! Can it be? . . . a mountain . . . coming down our throats?

Instinctively, he banged the crow's nest bell three times, warning of impending danger ahead for the vessel. At that moment the Titanic was bearing down on a wall of blue jagged ice that dropped vertically below the waterline.[1]

As often as I hear of the Titanic, I cannot shake from my mind the fear and confusion that Fleet must have felt in the crow's nest on that tragic evening. The responsibility of one man to protect, guard, and look out for the vessel under him had to have been an extremely stressful task.

I assure you, this is not another in-depth and detailed discourse on the life and sinking of the Titanic. I'll leave that to the local bookstore, which is full of books on this catastrophic event. What I want to draw our attention to is one of the most crucial roles of any seaman who has sailed on any vessel—Titanic or otherwise. I'm talking about the role of the one placed in the crow's nest.

The person we place in the crow's nest will determine how effectively our vessel is going to forge through the waters of life, navigating us toward home. When our wife, kids, career, and destiny are at stake, we don't want someone in the crow's nest second guessing what obstacles are coming our way. You and I need someone looking over our vessel who is stable, reliable, and can see a great distance even in the midst of the storms of life.

If Frederick Fleet could comment on that tragic night, I think he would ask a very poignant question. If the person in the crow's nest was responsible for taking the vessel to safe passage, why on earth was he not given a $14.95 pair of binoculars? Great question.

As we look over the condition of our lives, are we willing to risk and jeopardize our faith, family, and friends, by putting someone in the crow's nest who needs to squint in order to see what icebergs lay ahead? Not a chance!

Let's begin with a series of questions:

1. Whom can we trust enough to faithfully and dependably stand in the crow's nest when our vessel is forging into troubled waters?

2. Whom do we know that can loyally keep watch and not abandon his post or vessel under any circumstance?

3. If we want to be men whose coordinates are fixed and secure in order to lead our ship to lasting peace in a safe harbor, are we going to throw just anyone or anything in the nest only to fill a void?

4. When the squalls of life are bearing down, when the winds begin to change and the nights are so cold and the days are so hot we want to run for shelter, who's going to watch our vessel through it all?

Let's grab a pair of binoculars for a moment and see who we *cannot* afford to put in this position.

• Maybe we see *our family* taking the post in the crow's nest. As obedient, righteous, and God-fearing as I'm sure they are, forget it. They're not qualified enough for the position. Our children are apprentices and our wife holds the position of first mate with all of the responsibilities that position entails.

• How about *our career*? Sure, maybe today it's secure; stock in the company is climbing. But what happens tomorrow, next month, or next year when we are pulled into our boss's office and we hear the dreaded word—*downsizing*.

• How about *ourselves*? As strong, determined, and up for the job as we might think we are, there needs to be someone greater and stronger watching our lives. Someone who knows the interior and exterior of our body, soul, and spirit even better than ourselves. You and I cannot stand at the helm of our vessel sailing effectively and also be in the crow's nest. It's just not gonna happen.

• How about *our financial condition*? Do we really think our income or that stock portfolio we keep our eye on will enable us to push through life with no problems? Maybe for a season, but when the waves of life are tossing us around, money is not going to keep us afloat, nor save our soul. Remember the words of Jesus:

> *What good is it for a man to gain the whole world, yet forfeit his soul?* (Mark 8:36)

Then there's the wisdom of Solomon:

> *Whoever loves money never has money enough; whoever loves wealth is never satisfied with his income* (Ecclesiastes 5:10).

Who is earnestly willing and wanting to stand in that position and see us through every stormy squall, every windy day, every sunrise and sunset? Let me give you a hint:

> *For the eyes of the Lord range throughout the earth to strengthen those whose hearts are fully committed to him* (2 Chronicles 16:9).

O Lord, you have searched me and you know me. You know when I sit and when I rise; you perceive my thoughts from afar. You discern my going out and my lying down, you are familiar with all my ways (Psalm 139:1-3).

The One who stands in the crow's nest and *looks out for you, looks down on you,* and *looks in on you* must be Jesus Christ! Anyone or anything other than the perfect, sinless Son of the living God, as the one who stands watch, puts our family, future, and us on a collision course for shipwreck.

In order for us to experience lasting peace and significance, we must have clear and unmistakable coordinates to navigate toward (2 Timothy 2:21). We need Christ to stand watch, assuring us of safe travel so that we can reach our appointed destination.

That doesn't mean that it will be easy, nor always fun. Nor does it mean that we won't experience some pain and grief along the way. But it does guarantee that He will never leave nor abandon His post in our life because He has our best interest in mind.

We're just beginning our journey, but before we start out we need to share a few basic "rules of the sea" such as:

• We must acknowledge and be conscious of the fact that Christ wants to stand watch over our lives. Not just for tonight, not just in a jam at work or in a marital or parental squabble. He wants to be placed up there and acknowledged for all time.

• He wants to be Lord—every day, not just when it's convenient, or when our sails are full and we're clipping through life without a problem.

• He wants to be our friend. He seeks to come to our aid and minister to us throughout the day. "Greater love has no one than this, that he lay down his life for his friends" (John 15:13).

A man who fails to put Christ at the foremast of his vessel will struggle in finding lasting peace throughout his journey in life.

What does Christ seek to do in the crow's nest when we place Him there permanently? The next several chapters will help us in practical ways as we begin to navigate our hearts toward the understanding that our identity must lie solely in Christ.

As we seek to navigate our lives according to the coordinates of God's Word, we become instinctively mindful that He is watching and wanting to help us in the midst of our day.

➤ CHARTING YOUR COURSE ➤

SELF-EVALUATION

1. Where might you find it difficult to trust the Lord in situations that you feel capable of handling yourself?

2. At work, or when you are out and about, mentally begin to observe how people strive to achieve a lasting peace and purpose to life.

3. Read 2 Chronicles 16:9; Psalm 139:1-12; and Isaiah 26:3-4. Determine the following:
    A. Who have you placed in the crow's nest of your vessel to guide and direct your course?
    B. Who do you place in the crow's nest when things are going well? What about when you're going through confusion, pain, or heartache due to life's struggles?

4. What do you see or not see in your life that indicates that your identity and purpose for life is rooted in Him? (See Colossians 2:6.)

GROUP DISCUSSION

1. What kind of character traits do you look for in a friend? Do any of these match up to the friendship Christ offers to us without reservation? (See Proverbs 17:17; 18:24; and John 15:9-17.)

2. Discuss Jesus' statement in John 15:5, "Apart from Me you can do nothing." How does this verse shed light on your dependency on Christ? What do you depend on Him for?

3. Where do men strive to find lasting identity and significance in life? What are the positive and negative aspects to these?

Video Resource: An excellent resource for group discussion on personal identity and purpose is the video entitled *Search for Significance* in the "Guard Your Heart" series by Dr. Gary Rosberg of Cross Trainers Ministries. The video runs about 30 minutes.

Cross Trainer Ministries • 2540 106th Street, Suite 101
Des Moines, IA 50322 • (515) 334-7482 or 1-888-Rosberg

Music Resource: "Set Sail" by Ray Boltz on his *Allegiance* album is an excellent way to conclude your group discussion. The song keys in on setting sail on life's journey by drawing on the strength and guidance of the Captain's (Lord's) calling.

Sources

[1] Charles Pellegrino, *Her Name*, Titanic, New York, New York: Avon Books, 1988, pp.20-21.

Chapter 3
THE MORNING WATCH

He Looks Out for You

Remember as a kid those long road trips taken with your parents? Those were memorable times my family had together. But as Dad shares with me now, for him they were long days and nights of striving to keep alert at the steering wheel.

With our luggage in tow, Mom and Dad would load the car in the middle of the night so we could get an early start. Blankets and pillows in hand ("Just in case you get tired," Mom would say), my sister and I would climb into the back seat of our parents' 1969 car and act like any seven and eight year old on their way to sunny Florida. We were on our way for a week of playing in the ocean, building sand castles, and going to Disney World.

Twenty minutes into the trip, we would ask Dad that irritating question, "Are we there yet?" For an hour or two we would be wired—playing, singing, and shoving each other until our eyelids were as heavy as anchors.

We gave little thought to the traffic going by, little thought of road signs or when we needed fuel. But Dad didn't. He was at his post, vigilantly keeping watch, driving us right on schedule toward our destination. Soon our eyes slammed shut, and we were clutching those blankets in a deep sleep. As we slept, we could rest assured that when we woke in the morning, Dad would still be awake (maybe a little red-eyed) at his post. He was faithfully looking out and making sure that we were secure and watched over. Why? Because looking out for us was a demonstration of his overwhelming commitment and love for us. And so it is with Christ! He is at His post, looking out over a new day that He has planned especially for you. Why? Because He loves you!

What's your morning like? If you're like most men, you roll out of bed and before your feet even hit the floor, you automatically think of one thing—the day ahead! Sound familiar? You can feel the stress of deadlines, confrontations, and hectic schedules as you shuffle your way to the bathroom. Things to do, people to see, commitments to keep, and quotas to fill.

I've said it over a thousand times, "When is it going to end? When is the rat race of life going to slow down so I can take a breath and eventually play catch up? When can I enjoy this journey called life rather than be enslaved to it?"

We have a saying posted in our office: "God put me on earth to accomplish a certain number of things. Right now, I am so far behind I will never die." Ever feel that way?

How many times have you looked in the bathroom mirror or guzzled down a cup of lukewarm coffee as you pulled up anchor and commuted to your second home (for some, it's become our first home—ouch!), consumed with the events that lay ahead for the day? (I must confess I've got my hand raised—guilty as charged.) And yet He watches and waits, looking out for you.

As you think about work…He thinks about you.

When you're thinking about the impossible juggling act you're going to need to perform to get it all done this morning, He's thinking about and looking out for you. When you don't think you can take another minute of the dog-eat-dog, scratch, and claw your way up the corporate ladder, He's watching and looking out for you.

When you forget about Him, He still thinks about you!

Why? Because His job is simple and well-defined during His morning watch—to look out for you. And that, my friend, never changes. Remember who we're talking about here. Jesus Christ is the same yesterday and today and forever (Hebrews 13:8).

He has one purpose, one goal, one love, one ambition, and one thought: to equip the individual He's watching over to be useful and set apart for Himself.

> *Therefore, if a man cleanses himself from these things, he will be a vessel for honor, sanctified, useful to the Master, prepared for every good work* (2 Timothy 2:21 NASB).

Mind boggling, isn't it? Don't you wish life could be that easy? It can be when you and I remember Who stands alert and strong in the crow's nest.

Just breathe in that morning air for a moment and take that thought in. Before you even wipe the sleep from your eyes, find a parking space, reach the office, or get to the site, He's looking over your morning and planning how to grow you in His character as you forge through those early morning hours.

Breathe in the prayer of David in the Psalms:

> *I lift up my eyes to the hills—where does my help come from? My help comes from the Lord, the Maker of heaven and earth.*

He will not let your foot slip—He who watches over you will not slumber; indeed, He who watches over Israel will neither slumber nor sleep. The Lord watches over you—the Lord is your shade at your right hand; the sun will not harm you by day, nor the moon by night. The Lord will keep you from all harm—He will watch over your life; the Lord will watch over your coming and going both now and forevermore (see Psalm 121:1-8).

While our work and agenda for the day may change, Christ doesn't. Isaiah 55:8-9 tells us that His ways are not our ways. I am so glad about that because the days I try to do it alone, in my own strength, forgetting to acknowledge that He is looking out for me, I will most certainly steer off course. I'll forget that my identity is in Christ, and my overall purpose in life is to bring glory to the Father. Remember 2 Chronicles 16:9:

> *For the eyes of the Lord range throughout the earth to strengthen those whose hearts are fully committed to Him.*

Did you catch that? Our heavenly Father, the Creator of the land

and the sea, is looking out over the earth and wanting to strengthen us. Yet there are some of us who will lean more on the wisdom of this world, thinking it will suffice in providing the strength and inner peace we long for, rather than leaning on the everlasting arms of the wisdom and power of God. (See Deuteronomy 33:27; Psalm 18: 32-33; and 139:23-24.)

Don't let the fact that God is watching out for you bring fear. It should bring great comfort and reassurance. If God is that concerned about your life and wants to provide His strength and power, how much more should we be faithful in the responsibilities He brings our way!

What's the answer then, when we're running a mad dash during those morning hours to fill our lives with purpose and identity? The answer is switching our value system to one that has stood the test of time: a biblical one that works. That can only be found through one Person. Not your boss, kids, parents, or even you. It's in knowing Christ personally.

You and I derive meaning and identity from understanding who we are in Christ. It's a position we occupy and a calling that's worth living for. My existence is not linked to any fame, fortune, or power I may have. No, I exist because the very nature of God enables me to be an image bearer of His Son. The destiny you and I choose is determined by our willingness, or lack thereof, to set biblical coordinates that will direct us towards biblical living, not worldly ambitions.

The problem comes when we think that our happiness is based on how our day went at work. If our day was extremely interesting and productive, we arrive home in an elated state. If our day was a bummer, we show up depressed. Our mood is based on circumstances rather than on keeping in step with the Spirit. There is a thread of truth that our identity is marked by our occupation, but here's where having our identity solely in our work, family, or tangibles breaks down. If what you do is who you are, then who are you when you don't do what you do anymore? When we base our personal worth on people, places, things, or circumstances, we will be disappointed. They will eventually let us down, become boring or break, and we will once again try to pursue something that will elevate our sense of purpose to a higher level of personal identity.

Craig Keener in the *Spirit at Work* says,

The Spirit reminds us whose we really are. Sometimes I get so wrapped up in what God has called me to do that I forget the most important part of my identity. Then the Spirit softly whispers the Father's words to my heart afresh: "My child..."[1]

Can I encourage and challenge you for a moment? Tomorrow morning when you roll out of bed, and your feet are racing before you even get them planted, ask the Lord this:

"Jesus Christ, Son of the Living God, as You look out for me on this morning watch . . .

". . . What would You have me become today?

". . . What would You have me do today?

". . . With whom would You have me share the Good News?

". . . How might You develop deeper character in me?

"Let me use this day and the days ahead, whether at work, leisure, or when I'm doing that lawn care I dread so much, to realize and acknowledge that You are building me into a stronger vessel to the glory of Your Father. Amen."

When you and I acknowledge that He has our best interests in mind, we are freed to live the abundant life we read about in John 10:10. Abundant living comes when Christ becomes our motivating factor. We then live life on the basis of His grace and sufficiency rather than unrealistic expectations others tend to place on us for personal achievement.

Consider the great hymn of faith...

WITHOUT HIM

Without Him I could do nothing,
Without Him I'd surely fail;
Without Him I would be drifting
Like a ship without a sail.
Jesus, O Jesus!
Do you know Him today?
Do not turn Him away.
O Jesus, O Jesus,
Without Him how lost I would be.[2]

If Christ is not in the crow's nest during the morning watch, then no matter how financially rewarding things might be throughout the day, the payoff just doesn't cut it. When you and I are too self-sufficient, self-dependent, and self-determined, we are consuming the formula for self-destruction. I know of men who have become so consumed with their job, hobbies, and even their sin, that they have shipwrecked themselves. They've been too prideful and arrogant to listen to and heed the instructions of the Lord.

What we're often consumed with throughout the day is usually revealed by our behavior. That behavior almost always becomes evident in those morning hours.

Here are a few things Christ is doing in the crow's nest on His morning watch as He looks out for us. May they be our first thought when we roll out of the sack, rather than the furthest thing from our minds.

- He is watching and alert (Psalm 145:20).
- He never grows tired, nor will He abandon the vessel that lays beneath Him (Psalm 121:3; Isaiah 40:28-31).
- He sees the temptations, enemy, and struggles on the horizon and wishes to change our course. Will we let Him? (See Proverbs 15:3.)
- He sees all (Proverbs 5:21).

OUTLOOK

To look around is to be distressed.
To look within is to be depressed.
To look to God is to be blessed.
Look at self and be disappointed.
Look at others and be discouraged.
Look at Christ and be satisfied.[3]
—*Author Unknown*

 CHARTING YOUR COURSE

SELF-EVALUATION

1. What do you find consuming you in the morning hours? How does it affect your attitude and actions?

2. How will Psalm 37:3-9 and Proverbs 4:18-19 bring comfort and a

brighter outlook on life when you step out into the world tomorrow morning?

3. What struggles or victories do you have during those morning hours?

4. When you think of Christ looking out for you, does that bring fear and embarrassment or comfort and reassurance? Why?

5. During the morning hours at work, school, wherever, how conscious are you that God is looking out for you? Often? Rarely? Why?

GROUP DISCUSSION
1. How can you bring glory to the Father at your workplace or wherever you go in those early morning hours? (See Psalms 63:3-5; 69:30.)

2. How can identifying ourselves in Christ help us in the early morning rush?

Video Resource: *The Tom Papania Story: From Mafia to Minister.* As an abused New York street punk of 15 years of age, Tom's main goal in life was to make Al Capone look like an amateur. An excellent video on what men try to fill their lives with in order to find lasting significance and purpose in life. A gripping video of how Tom worked his way up in organized crime to a trusted position in the New York Gambino crime family until Christ got ahold of his heart, and everything started to change. You will be talking about this video for a long time. Video can be purchased through:

God's Saving Grace Ministries • P.O. Box 756
Powder Springs, GA. 30073 • (770) 590-8775

Sources
[1] Craig Keener, "Spirit at Work," *Discipleship Journal*: Issue 91.

[2] Mylon R. LeFevre, *The Hymnal for Worship and Celebration*-song "Without Him," Waco, Texas: Word Music; LeFevre-Sing Publishing Co., Smyrna, Georgia, 1963, p.332.

[3] Eleanor Doan, *Speakers Sourcebook*: Grand Rapids, Michigan: Zondervan Publishing House, 1960, p.179.

Chapter 4
HIGH NOON

He Looks Down On You

I love westerns. There is nothing better than a good gun slinger movie to get me salivating, especially one with my hero—Clint Eastwood. *The Good, the Bad and the Ugly; A Fistful of Dollars; High Plains Drifter*—they don't get any better. You name them, I've probably watched them.

It never fails, sometime during a western there's going to be a gunfight. You can count on it; it's inevitable. A ruckus begins in the local tavern and before you know it, threats are being made. And you hear that familiar phrase, "I'll see you at high noon!" That only means one thing—a good old-fashioned gunfight.

Why high noon? Was it because that's the only time these ruffians could fit in a gunslinger battle due to their work schedule? Or was it because that was the best time of the day to bake in the hot sun and get a well-balanced tan as they faced each other in the middle of town? No, pardner! It was because everyone from town could come out and watch a shoot'em up showdown unfold.

I can see it now. They walk to the center of town, each man with sweat on his brow, a scruffy beard, and the stench of sweat. Silence hovers over the town. The best place to see such an event is not on the streets. No way, mister. Too easy to get shot yourself. Best place to be is on a balcony overlooking the action so nothing and nobody obstructs your vision. You have a perfect view of the fight without the worry of being distracted, or worse yet, becoming injured yourself. The two gunslingers stop and try to stare each other down. In a split second, the shots ring out and it's all over.

Right in the middle of our day, when the heat is on and things couldn't be more intense, Jesus Christ looks down from the heavenlies on you and me. And you know what? Nothing obstructs His vision; nothing gets in His way. He sees all, observes all. He has full view when the enemy wants to "take us out" right in the middle of the action. If the enemy thinks he can do that at high noon, he's gonna try it.

One of the places where he's going to try to pick us off or cause us to lose our perspective is at work. You know the feeling. It's noon (time for lunch), and you are up to your ears in work. That work is having you for lunch. Things are in full swing at the daily grind. All systems go. But what about you? You're tired, irritable, short with people, and in desperate need of a vacation. "Anywhere," you say. "Just get me away from the phones, faxes, and beeper messages before I am driven to insanity!"

Wolfgang Hasselhus in *Collision and Liability* says,

> As long as God's will lines up with our own wishes, everything is fine with us. But when our personal goals collide with God's will, we truly learn what His lordship over us means. God calls us to give Him not the sum total of the little things we happen to have a surplus of, but that which is most strongly connected with our personal identity—the things with which our very life is entwined.[1]

It's right in the midst of our day when things become most urgent that we discover how much of our identity is tied up in our work or in trying to get ahead financially. Has your workplace deceived you into believing that your company will never make it or survive another day until you sacrifice all for the "good" of the company? Or maybe you have bought into the lie that financial success is the way to personal fulfillment and happiness.

In a yearly study sponsored by the American Council on Education and conducted by UCLA's Educational Research Institute, 75 percent of the college freshmen in 1987 considered "being well off financially" as an "essential" or "major life goal." When financial success becomes the controlling goal of life, it usually skews a person's whole value system, bringing devastating results.

Michael Korda writes in *Success*,

> It's O.K. to be greedy. It's O.K. to be ambitious. It's O.K. to look out for Number One. It's O.K. to have a good time. It's O.K. to recognize that honesty is not always the best policy. It's O.K. to be a winner. And, it's always O.K. to be rich.[2]

His conflict with Christian values is obvious. Although the Bible never has a problem with wealth, it warns against the stranglehold misplaced priorities can have on our lives. Remember Paul's warning in 1 Timothy 6:9-10 against getting entrapped by the pursuit and enticement of riches?

People who are desperate to get rich don't resist the temptation to fulfill many foolish and harmful desires that eventually plunge them into ruin and destruction. For the *love of* money is the root of all kinds of evil. Some people, eager for money, have wandered from the faith and pierced themselves with many griefs.

"The critical issue is not *whether* we've set our heart on something, but *what* we have set it on, and *how* we are pursuing it."[3] Have you in some way identified yourself by a lucrative lifestyle of financial success? If you have, what will become of your identity when you go through a season of financial hardship or even debt?

It's time for a sanity check. Forget the phone, forget the order that came down 10 minutes ago and needed to be on the dock for shipping 20 minutes ago, and consider: If you think you are indispensable and your company can't function without you, put your finger in a glass of water...pull it out, and see what kind of hole you leave. Pretty humbling isn't it? Well, the next time high noon rolls around, let's remember the following as we seek to navigate our life through God's Word:

1. When we think about fudging the figures to make them fit, think

again. Let's choose integrity over dishonest gain. (See Proverbs 10:9; 11:3.)

2. When the temptation is to "innocently" ask that new, attractive receptionist out for dinner, remember this—the Lord sees your wedding ring and will take no part in that meal. He knows what "Last Suppers" are like.

3. When we begin to entertain thoughts of cutting corners on the project to save a few bucks, think about the parable in Luke 14:28-30 that might stimulate a more godly decision.

4. When we move the decimal point on our expense report to justify playing golf on company time—He's watching. (Besides, some of our golf games need more than justifying.)

I like the way Solomon put it:

For a man's ways are in full view of the Lord, and He examines all his paths (Proverbs 5:21).

Men, if we're going to be pure and set apart for Christ, then it's going to take more than a good *talk* to make it happen. It's going to have to be a *walk* that will last our entire life. It's going to take more than *telling* other Christians at the office that you're putting Christ first, when your *living* (temper, ego, language—that's enough) and character say otherwise.

The humorous story is told of how a United Airlines flight had been canceled. People where standing in a long line to see how they could catch a connecting flight to their next destination. There was only one agent working behind the ticket counter at the time, trying to deal with the many questions and concerns of all the people whose flight had been canceled. One angry passenger pushed himself in front of everybody else. He got to the counter and said to the agent, "I have to be on this next flight, and it has to be first class!" The agent said, "Very well sir, but you are going to have to wait your turn in line and then I will be happy to assist you when it's your turn." The passenger was livid. In a loud voice for everybody to hear, he said, "Do you have any idea who I am?" Whereupon the quick agent, without hesitation, picked up the public address microphone for the whole terminal, and said, "May I have your attention please, we have a passenger here at Gate 4 who does not know who he is. If anyone can help him find his identity please come to the gate."[4]

People are struggling with an identity crisis today. The three questions men are asking themselves are:

1. Who am I? *A question of identity.*

2. What should I believe? *A question of ideology.*

3. How do I relate with others? *A question of interpersonal relationships.*

First Corinthians 6:19-20 tells us exactly who we are in Jesus Christ:

> *Do you not know that your body is a temple of the Holy Spirit who is in you, whom you have received from God? For you are not your own, you were bought at a price. Therefore honor God with your body.*

Gary Rosberg, in his book, *Guard Your Heart,* puts it this way,

> The bottom-line question in God's eternal kingdom is not *who* you are, but *whose* you are. It's not what you have, but who has you. It's not what you've accomplished, but what Jesus has accomplished on your behalf. It's not the praise and admiration of men, but the grace and acceptance of God. It's not what you've acquired, but what you've surrendered.

> You and I don't have to perform to be accepted. He accepts us with our flaws. It's because of our flaws and our inability to hit the mark that God sent His Son to die for us. Yes, He wants us to do well to bring honor to Him, but our identity is sealed by a relationship, not a performance. The how part of our significance is answered by our simple acceptance of Him and His role in our life as Lord.[5]

Here are some favorite bullets of mine that I always ask God to fire my way when things get a little sticky at "high noon," and I tend to forget who I am as a vessel for Christ.

1. Have I not commanded you? Be strong and courageous. Do not

be terrified; do not be discouraged, for the Lord your God will be with you wherever you go (Joshua 1:9).

2. Whatever you do, work at it with all your heart, as working for the Lord, not for men (Colossians 3:23).

3. Let your conversation be always full of grace, seasoned with salt, so that you may know how to answer everyone (Colossians 4:6).

4. Therefore, my dear brothers, stand firm. Let nothing move you. Always give yourselves fully to the work of the Lord, because you know your labor in the Lord is not in vain (1 Corinthians 15:58).

5. A simple man believes anything, but a prudent man gives thoughts to his steps (Proverbs 14:15).

Men, at high noon there are two things you can count on. . .The sun is directly overhead, and the Son is directly overhead!

CHARTING YOUR COURSE

SELF-EVALUATION

1. At a business luncheon or a social gathering with your spouse, listen to the conversations going on at various tables. How would you categorize the depth of what they are saying?
   A. Shallow or boring?
   B. Stimulating or thought provoking?
   C. Building/edifying?
   D. Destructive/depressing?

2. How much of your identity do you think is wrapped up in who gets the glory? (Selfish ambitions or God-centered living?)

3. It's lunch time! What's on the menu of conversation with your peers?
   A. Complaining about work?
   B. Disrespectful or negative comments about a co-worker, spouse or friend?
   C. Encouragement, affirmation, positive spiritual overtones, or discussion?

D. The shape and walk of the waitress that is taking your order?
E. The weather and sports?
F. Other?
How might the conversation be improved tomorrow at high noon?

4. How much of your identity is placed in your job?
   A. Does it consume you?
   B. Does it grab and occupy your attention even when at home or on vacation?
   C. Does your family really come before your job? Or is that a saying you use to ease the guilty conscience you feel?

5. How much of your identity is placed in *what you own*? Do you spend money you don't have, on things you don't need, to impress people you don't know?

6. How much of your identity is placed in *who you know*? Do you surround yourself with or drop the names of popular people you know to impress others? Are your relationships truly genuine, or are they surface and superficial?

7. How much of your identity is placed in *what you make*? Do you find a way to impress others in conversation by bringing up: recent raises; how much interest your retirement plan is getting; the price of your car, house, etc.; your current salary or latest bonus?

GROUP DISCUSSION
1. How can developing an improper identity cause us to drift from the coordinates of God's Word?

2. What warning signs can you establish in your life in keeping a proper God-centered identity?

Video Resource: Dr. Gene Neill was a professional race car driver, and he served honorably in the United States Marine Corps in the Far East during the Korean War. Having graduated with a Doctorate in Law, cum laude, from the University of Miami School of Law, he served as a Public Defender in Miami for three years. Later, Dr. Neill was appointed as a Prosecuting Attorney in Miami, where he prosecuted many of the organized crime and Mafia figures in the East Coast underworld. Finally he became a very successful criminal defense attorney in Miami. When he was 40, Neill became deeply involved in organized crime and was sentenced to serve 50 years in a Federal penitentiary. But in a little dimly-lit underground solitary isolation cell, Gene had a dramatic conversion experience.

Gene Neill's story is one you do not want to miss. It will grip your heart and move you to live a life for God. His powerful video and best-selling book, *I'm Gonna' Bury You,* can be purchased by contacting:

World Wide Prison Ministries • Post Office Box 78

Mayo, Florida 32066

(http://www.go-to-jail.org)

Music Resource: "Busy Man" by Steven Curtis Chapman on his *For the Sake of the Call* CD.

Sources

[1] Wolfgang Hasselkus, "Collision and Liability," *Discipleship Journal,* Issue 5.

[2] Michael Korda, *Success,* New York: Random House, 1977, pp.4-5.

[3] Jerry Harvill, "Ambition: Vice or Virtue?" *Discipleship Journal,* Issue 58.

[4] *Great Stories,* Vol. 4/Issue 16, Oct./Nov. 1997.

[5] Dr. Gary Rosberg, *Guard Your Heart,* Questar Publishers, Inc. Sisters, Oregon, 1994, pp.141-142.

Chapter 5

FROM DUSK TILL DAWN

He Looks in on You

Jim is a true friend. He's watched my back and come to my rescue on many occasions. I appreciate who he is. We are friends; he loves the Lord, and I respect and admire him because he put his life on the line for me and for this country. You see, Jim is a veteran of the Vietnam War. A Radio Communications Specialist stationed in South Vietnam from 1969-1970. He pretty much saw it all. When we talk about it, I sense that he'd like to put it behind him and discuss something else. But what Jim shared with me in a van coming back from a trip to Pennsylvania one evening was frightful to hear. I can't imagine what it would have been like to experience. Jim tells it like this:

"I was given the station of 'listening post' that evening. That's where you find yourself outside of the base camp looking out over the perimeter for the enemy. So with my M-16 I took my post at dusk and became the eyes of the base behind me until dawn. My orders were simple: Protect at all cost! I can't explain how eerie it was sitting through the night and listening for what I could not see. I dared not move, for in doing so I might give up my position, or worse yet, get picked off by enemy intrusion. All throughout the night I felt bugs, snakes, and other creatures of the night crawl on me and slither past me. But I could not move. While those in base camp slept, I was burning the midnight oil protecting them from dusk till dawn."

When Jim shared his story, I wondered how it might be for my Savior, Jesus Christ, to faithfully look over His children, and guard the base of my life and family from the enemy from dusk till dawn. As I sleep, He watches, prays, and protects me from the evil one. What assurance, what comfort, what a Savior!

Tonight, instead of lying in bed and thinking about all that needs to be done tomorrow, remember—

> *You perceive my thoughts from afar. You discern my going out and my lying down, you are familiar with all my ways. If I rise on the wings of the dawn, if I settle on the far side of the sea, even there your hand will guide me* (Psalm 139:2-3,9-10; see also Psalm 113:3; 125:2).

Thank the Lord for watching the perimeter of your vessel. What an awesome God we serve!

HIS IDENTITY IS MY IDENTITY

Neil Anderson in his book, *Victory Over the Darkness*, gives an excellent list from Scripture of our true identity in Christ. You and I can't earn or buy these positions any more than a person born in America can earn or buy the rights and freedoms he enjoys as an American citizen. These traits are guaranteed to you by the Word of God simply because you were born into God's holy nation by placing your faith in Christ. Here are just a few of them:

WHO AM I?
- I am a child of God (John 1:12).
- I am Christ's friend (John 15:15).
- I am chosen and appointed by Christ to bear His fruit (John 15:16).
- I am a slave to righteousness (Romans 6:18).
- I am a joint heir with Christ, sharing His inheritance with Him (Romans 8:17).
- I am a member of Christ's body (1 Corinthians 12:27; Ephesians 5:30).
- I am a new creation (2 Corinthians 5:17).

- I am God's workmanship—His handiwork—born anew in Christ to do His work (Ephesians 2:10).
- I am chosen of God, holy and dearly loved (Colossians 3:12; 1 Thessalonians 1:4).
- I am a partaker of Christ; I share in His life (Hebrews 3:14).[1]

Understanding your identity in Christ is absolutely essential to your success at living the Christian life. No person can consistently behave in a way that's inconsistent with the way he perceives himself. If you think you're a no-good bum, you'll probably live like a no-good bum. But if you see yourself as a child of God who is spiritually alive in Christ, you'll begin to live in victory and freedom as He lived. Next to a knowledge of God, a knowledge of who you are is by far the most important truth you can possess.[2]

KEEPING THE MAIN THING, THE MAIN THING

I am reminded of the simple but powerful words of Matthew 6:33,

But seek ye first the kingdom of God and His righteousness, and all these things will be added unto you (KJV).

Our work, family, goals, and dreams are all added things to that of seeking God. When the added things of life become our motivation for personal identity, we set ourselves up for disappointment. Seeking the kingdom of God and His righteousness must be the main thing. When Christ is the priority and reference point for living, all these "added things" will fall into place, provided we keep the right perspective.

I can think of no one who demonstrated the priority of pursuing Christ's agenda better than the great George Mueller, the Englishman renowned for his work with orphans. Someone once asked him how he could sustain such devoted service:

There was a day when I died. Died utterly; died to George Mueller, his opinions, preferences, tastes, and will—died to the world, its approval or censure—died to the approval or blame even of my brethren or friends—and since then I have studied only to show myself approved unto God.[3]

31

So, who or what has become the "main thing" in your life? If it's not Christ, it can be. Here's how. You must believe by faith that . . .

1. God loves you and has a special course planned out for your life. His plan is for you to know Him and live in His kingdom as you grow in a deep personal relationship with Him (John 3:16; Romans 5:1,5).

2. You are a sinner and your sin separates you from God. In your sinful condition you cannot know or experience God's plan for you. Sinful man is subject to Satan's power and destined to receive the same punishment as Satan—eternity in hell (Romans 3:23; 6:23).

3. God's Son, Jesus Christ, died for your sins by shedding His blood so you may have eternal life with Him. By Christ's death, burial, and resurrection, He defeated Satan and paid the debt that we owed for our sins (Romans 4:25; 1 Peter 3:18).

4. Receive Christ as Savior and Lord by confessing your sin and recognizing that you become a child of God and nothing can separate you from His love. It's through the confession and the repentance of your sins that you are reconciled to God the Father (Romans 10:9-10; 1 John 1:9; 5:11-12).

5. Begin to grow in His Word and live for Him. You are now a new creation in Christ. He will give you the power through His Spirit to live righteously and victoriously in Christ (1 Corinthians 15:56-57; 2 Corinthians 5:17).

Jackie Robinson was the first black baseball player to break the color barrier in major league baseball. In every city he went, he was jeered and taunted because of his color. In fact, in front of his own home crowd, his own stadium, they would scoff at him. On one occasion, Robinson had made an error at second base, and the crowd began to boo and yell sarcastic remarks at him. Pee Wee Reese was playing short stop. In that moment when it seemed like Jackie was up against tremendous odds and felt like he didn't have a friend in the world, Pee Wee Reese left his position, stood beside Jackie Robinson and put his arm around him. Jackie later said, "It was that one gesture of love and friendship that saved my career."[4]

And so it is with Christ. He left His post and came to our aid. He not only ministers to us today, but gave His very life so we might stay on course for every tomorrow as we allow Him to navigate our lives toward biblical manhood.

CHARTING YOUR COURSE

SELF-EVALUATION

1. In what ways does the Lord pray for you, as He watches the perimeter of your life and family? (See Romans 8:27,34; Hebrews 9:25.)

2. How might the enemy "prey" on you as he seeks to find a weak spot in the perimeter of your life?

3. Commit to memorizing for this next week Psalm 113:3 and Psalm 125:2.

GROUP DISCUSSION

1. How do the traits by Neil Anderson encourage and strengthen you in understanding your identity as a child of God?

2. Testimonial Resource: Find a man in your church or men's ministry who served in Vietnam. Have him share what it was like to experience combat. What did he learn about the enemy? Was he ever in a situation where he had to put his life on the line for his platoon?

Sources
[1] Neil T. Anderson, *Victory Over The Darkness*, Ventura, California: Regal Books, 1990, pp.45-47.

[2] *Ibid*. pp.43-44.

[3] George Mueller, reprint of "An Hour with George Mueller: The Man to Whom God Gave Millions" in *George Mueller Man of Faith* (Grand Rapids: Zondervan), p.52.

[4] Alfred Duckett, *I Never Had It Made; Told by Jackie Robinson-Autobiography of Jackie Robinson*, G.P. Putnam's Sons, New York, New York, 1972, pp.76-77.

COORDINATE #2

Navigating
Toward
Spiritual Maturity

Chapter 6
LONGITUDE LIVING

When you can't change the direction of the wind,
adjust your sails. —Max DePree

I felt like I had just been punched in the stomach. I was sitting with a trusted friend over breakfast several years ago. Our conversation drifted in and out over weather, sports, our ministry, wives, and children. Things were going well as we asked surface questions regarding one another. Eventually the discussion turned to what the Lord had been teaching us through His Word. We shared for what seemed to be 10-15 minutes. Then out from nowhere I got blindsided. I didn't see it coming. He looked straight into my eyes and said, "Craig, are you a skimmer?"

"A what?" I asked.

"A skimmer," he said again. He explained. "When you pick up a Christian book to read, do you skim past the Bible references thinking you already know them and press on to what the author really has to say?"

I just sat there trying to look innocent.

He continued, "Do you find yourself doing the same when reading the Word of God? Do you skim past the verses that bring conviction or admonish you to change in a particular way, and zero in only on the verses that bring comfort or personal affirmation for your soul?" My face and body felt numb, like a boxer who had been relentlessly pummeled with no sense of feeling left. I thought, *What do I say? Do I lie and put on the self-righteous mask and make it sound like I have my act together, that my time in the Word is never missed and my reading of the Word is extremely thorough?* But the best I could conjure up at that moment was a sheepish and embarrassed, "Yes."

I learned through that conversation and over the years in my walk with Christ, that if I truly desire to be God's man, doing God's business in order to bring God glory, I must resist every temptation to skim over the spiritual disciplines required by Scripture.

In this chapter we want to examine the longitude* (vertical) relationship we have with Christ, [*longitude*—*although longitude is figured as degrees east and west, it is most commonly thought of in vertical terms, hence we use the word longitude in this chapter and latitude in the next one*] and then in the next chapter identify how these affect our latitude (horizontal) relationships with others.

The best way to determine how much spiritual progress we are making is to use the sailing term "tacking" as a means of charting our course toward biblical manhood. *Tacking* is a procedure that a sailor will use to maneuver his vessel from point A to point B. He knows that the destination that lies ahead cannot be reached by sailing straight into the wind, for he will make little, if any, progress. So, like switchbacks on a mountain slope too steep to ascend directly, he will angle his sails, zigzagging, or "tacking," from left to right causing the wind to fill the sail, all the while moving him closer to the intended object or destination he has charted.

Here are three tacking maneuvers that will help us in charting our spiritual maturity along the way.

Tacking Maneuver #1
THE WORD OF GOD

Reading, meditating, and memorizing the Word of God will be our greatest strength toward righteousness and our best defense against sinful living. When we avoid this tacking maneuver, we are thrown completely off course. The end result will be a weakened condition whereby we become vulnerable to the flesh, Satan, and the world's lifestyle. We need to be navigating our spiritual lives through the Word of truth so we can walk worthy of the calling we have received (see Ephesians 4:1).

Our relationship with the Lord often becomes confused, unbalanced, even rigid, due to the unrealistic expectations and pressures we place on ourselves and others place on us to read the Word. I am glad when people encourage me to read, memorize, meditate, and practically apply the truth of God's Word. I love to read the Word of God and see it as a priority for every man, woman, and child who desires to grow in the grace and knowledge of Jesus Christ. If we are to be men of integrity, a steady diet of the Word of God is a must for developing traits consistent with biblical manhood.

The problem arises, however, when the expectations others try to place on us become more demanding than those asked of us by the Lord. Glances of disapproval are apparent when we humbly confess before others we didn't have the best week devoted to the Word of God. Feelings of regret, judgment, and guilt cause us to question our relationship with Christ. We feel that in some way we don't have our lives together like others appear to have. The result, many times, will be that we drop out of the race because "we just didn't have what it took to please God." This kind of guilt trip from others, we can do without.

Our longitudinal relationship with Christ is never to be based on how many times per week we can crank out a quiet time with Him. I believe it's based on a heart that steadily maneuvers closer to the Lord through the seasons of life. Godly character and discipline will not be forged in our lives overnight, but over a period of time. Growth is a *process* not an event, and usually comes at a glacial pace rather than a mad dash toward holiness.

I remember my father teaching me to play golf at the age of eight. We would load up our clubs (okay, Dad would do the loading, I would just watch) and head out to this old run-down golf course in farm country. I remember how frustrated I would get when I would watch my father pull a driver out of his bag and knock a 275-yard drive straight down the middle of the fairway. I would then turn to grab my driver. But my father would always say, "In time, son. You're not old enough or strong enough to use that club yet." And with a smile he would hand me a nine iron. I remember trying with all my might to hit that nine iron shot out to where my Dad's golf ball laid. But it didn't happen then. It was going to take years of discipline and maturity (which I'm still acquiring, by the way). I wouldn't become a great golfer overnight. It took practice, hundreds of hours on the golf range, and a keen ear listening to the instructions of a loving father in order to see progress. There were days I wanted to give up and put away the clubs, feeling like little, if any, progress was being made. But I stayed with it and over the years as I improved, I began to see the blessing of sticking with something I love, rather than bailing out when things seemed too tough to go on. I grew stronger, wiser, and now can out drive my father. I'm so glad I listened and persevered.

When *doing* the things of God supersedes *being His son*, we can easily fall prey to a regimented and legalistic lifestyle rather than a relationship where we actively sense Christ is maneuvering us by His love and understanding in our pursuit of biblical manhood. We need to be cautious as well, that we do not find ourselves wallowing in the stagnant waters of apathy by avoiding, ignoring, or becoming spiritually lazy in making time to hear His voice. Our meeting with the Lord should be a privilege as we sit at His feet, listening without hurry to the what's, why's, where's, and how's of living.

True discipline of the Word is the maturing process which moves a man closer to the cross of Christ and causes him to fix his sights on Christ's kingdom agenda. Are there going to be days when we struggle to find time with God? You bet. Are there going to be days when you want to quit and hang it up? Sure there are. Are there going to be days, even weeks, where we feel like we are in a spiritual desert with nothing more than a hope and a prayer that this dryness will eventually turn into an oasis? Absolutely.

This journey we share with Christ is not always easy or clear. But maneuvering our life toward the Father by obeying His commands will never bring disappointment. We can trust the Captain of our soul to chart us a course that will fill our lives with more joy and praise than we could ever imagine (see Ephesians 3:14-21).

Blessed are they whose ways are blameless, who walk according to the law of the Lord. Blessed are they who keep His statutes and seek Him with all their heart. I will praise You with an upright heart as I learn Your righteous laws. How can a young man keep his way pure? By living according to Your word. I seek You with all my heart; do not let me stray from Your commands. I have hidden Your word in my heart that I might not sin against You. I run in the path of Your command, for You have set my heart free. Your statutes are my heritage forever; they are the joy of my heart. My heart is set on keeping Your decrees to the very end (Psalm 119:1-2,7, 9-11,32,111-112).

What I appreciate about my longitudinal (vertical) relationship with the Lord is that if I miss a day or two, He does not sit in heaven with a tablet and pencil crossing me off His list of faithful servants. We are going to have days when time flies by, schedules are hectic, and we wonder where the day went. "Every day is new and there are no mistakes in it." This is my favorite line from the movie *Anne of Green Gables.* Rather than beating ourselves up when we haven't read, prayed, or honored the Lord in some way, see it as a positive by recognizing that maturity and discipline is still being forged in our lives.

In 1937 David Mulligan joined the Winged Foot Golf Club in Westchester County, New York. After routinely reloading after hitting a poor drive, his friends began to label the second shot a "Mulligan." Thus the golf term, "Mulligan."[1] God gives us a new start, a "mulligan" if you will, every morning. That doesn't mean we take advantage of His grace and mercy. It does mean it's available to use without the fear or guilt with which the enemy readily tries to paralyze our soul. Let's maneuver our life every day by the Word of God.

Tacking Maneuver #2
PRAYER

If time spent with the Lord in His Word is a spiritual tacking maneuver moving us closer to the Father, then prayer has to be its counterpart. In his popular ballad, "My Eyes Are Dry," Keith Green sang about struggling with a hard heart and prayers that had grown cold.[2] Ever feel that way? I sure do from time to time. Sometimes our prayer life could be defined as inconsistent, distant, shallow, cold, routine, even passive. At other times it's invigorating, passionate, moving, and inspiring.

We want our prayer life to have depth and intimacy, but often it falls short of our hopes and we drift into settling for a nominal prayer life. What keeps a man from developing a heart to pray? I have narrowed it down to two reasons: fear and unwillingness to surrender.

As men, we have been raised to fear nothing. "You never back down, you never give up, you never give in, and you never show fear." We are taught from our early years of growing up that fear is a sign of weakness. If anything or anyone threatened us, we quickly learned to build a well fortified wall to protect ourselves from vulnerability. If we sensed any possible attack upon those self-constructed walls, it would make us feel uneasy or defensive. So we learned to keep a stern face to the wind and avoid anything that would threaten the thin veneer of our spiritual "appearance."

Praying involves exposing the inner soul. Transparency and dependency are required when we approach the throne of grace in prayer. This, however, can bring fear to the person who does not want to be vulnerable and open up, especially when it involves sharing pain or neediness. Prayer chips away at the self-dependency of a man and puts the focus on his dependency on God. Prayer reveals areas that are often extremely private or tender, which can cause a man to withdraw from its power rather than embrace it.

Prayer also brings fear of the unknown. We worry about what God might ask us to be, change, or do, which may not be penciled in on our agenda. We have the fear of taking our hands off the helm and letting Him lead us in ways we had not planned. It is easy to say we don't have time to pray or that we don't know what to say. Those excuses can become an easy way out so we don't have to face the reality that when we pray we have to depend on the Lord for strength and guidance. For many of us, that's very hard to do. It's very difficult to let go and let Him lead. We like to be in control of the situation. We want to supply the answer to life's ups and downs, rather than lean on the One who says He will supply all your needs (see Philippians 4:19). That's where surrender comes in.

Surrender has no "I" in it. But if you look close, you will see the word "end" in it. Through prayer, God wants to bring an end to the "I" in our life. We come into a greater vertical relationship with our heavenly Father through the fellowship of sharing our heart and thoughts openly with Him. That involves surrender to a higher power. It involves seeing Christ as the *first* option for help, rather than the *last* one before we go under.

For the man who just lost his job and wonders how the next month's bills are going to get paid—pour your heart out to the Father (Psalm 55:22; 1 Peter 5:7).

For the man struggling with sin—He's waiting, tell it like it is (James 5:16; 1 John 1:9).

For the husband and wife grieving over the miscarriage of their baby—God wants to wrap his arms around you as a child of God. Let Him do it through prayer (Psalm 34:18; Habakkuk 3:17-19).

For the husband and wife who just received news that she is pregnant after five long years of trying—Praise Him through prayer (Psalm 105:1-4; 113).

For the man striving to make correct personal decisions—let Him be your guide (Psalm 32:8; 48:14; Isaiah 28:26).

Let's keep praying, men. Let's not fall into the enemy's well disguised trap by having a mentality that says, "The Lord already knows what I'm going to ask before I say it, so why pray?" God is able to handle your situation far beyond any resources available to us on this earth. Don't let fear and pride keep you from coming to the throne of grace. A simple equation helps in seeing the priority prayer must have in our lives:

No prayer = No power
Little prayer = Little power
Much prayer = Much power

Do we have any greater resources available to us in this world to handle our situation than when we go to the throne of grace in our time of need? Never. Power and help come from the Lord's loving and comforting hands. Let us then approach the throne of grace with confidence, so that we may receive mercy and find grace to help us in our time of need (Hebrews 5:16).

Here is what prayer is going to do for us when we determine to stay on course and navigate towards biblical manhood: We will be changed in heart, body, and soul. Through prayer we begin to see spiritual progress in becoming the noble vessel He longs for us to be. We only lose our way when we cease to pray.

Tacking Maneuver #3
WORSHIP

Todd Blackledge, former quarterback for the Kansas City Chiefs and Pittsburgh Steelers, tells the story of when he played for the Penn State Lions.

"When game day came you could feel the intensity in the locker room. Some guys were quiet, and focused. Others were charged up and ready to go out and knock some heads. Still, some were found hugging the toilet because they were so nervous. As we would leave the locker room and head toward the filled-to-capacity stadium, we could hear the fans and band screaming and playing with every ounce of passion they had. The adrenaline we felt within was like a keg of dynamite ready to explode. As we walked through the tunnel and approached the field, we would cross over a blue line stretched the length of the walkway. The blue line represented two important truths to every football player on our team.

"One, it didn't matter what was going on in our personal lives—dating, school, family problems, whatever—the moment we stepped over that line and onto the field, it was left behind. There were to be no distractions. The only thing that was to be on our minds was the game. We had a job to do.

"Two, in crossing the blue line we knew we would never be the same. We either would be a more mature football team that day when we returned to the locker room, or a team that would learn some hard lessons about losing. But either way we would never be the same, and yet all the stronger from it." (See 1 Cor. 15:58; 1 Cor. 16:13.)

When you think of worship, is that what you experience? Do you cross over the threshold of grace, forgetting how lousy your week may have been, and focus your attention on one thing—your Lord and Savior Jesus Christ?

Let's worship His majesty and sing, praise, learn, and give honor with all the passion and joy our spirit can handle. The joy of laying aside anything that entangles us and setting our heart and mind on the Author and Perfecter of our faith is an act of loyalty to the Lord. When we worship privately or corporately, the only One that you and I should care about cheering us on is the Lord. How you and I worship demonstrates the overflow of His Word cutting through the thoughts and intentions of the heart (Hebrews 4:12). Focus on the Eternal One—His character, holiness, and guidance for living—so when we go back into the world this morning, tomorrow, or whenever, we are all the stronger for it. Let's keep in step with the Spirit, men, and not be ashamed of our Savior. Worship Him. He is worthy to be praised. Don't get hung up on the hows, whys, or why nots. Enter into His rest and be still knowing that He is God. Listen for His instructions so you will journey through life with a clear understanding of His voice and calling for you (See Psalm 29:1-2; 46:10; 48:1; 95:6-7).

If we intend to see spiritual maturity in our lives over the long haul, we must keep our eyes and heart fixed on Christ. Take a moment and place yourself under the "life grid" below. Ask God to sift your life through these questions as you examine your longitudinal relationship with Christ on a daily basis.

- What does my faith cost me? (1 Samuel 15:22; 2 Samuel 24:24)
- Where is the fruit in my life? (John 15:16)
- What is my first love? (Matthew 6:21; Revelation 2:1-7)
- Is there a flame in my heart for Christ? (2 Timothy 1:6)
- Does my worship flow continually throughout the week? (Matthew 12:35; John 4:23-24)
- Am I feared by Satan? (Luke 22:31-32; James 4:7-8)

CHARTING YOUR COURSE

SELF-EVALUATION

1. Do you feel guilty when you haven't read the Bible for a couple of days? Why is that? Is the guilt because of expectations others have placed on you, or the convicting power of the Holy Spirit?
2. Is it easier or harder to skip reading scripture today when you've missed it yesterday? Why?

3. What fears do you have that could keep you from surrendering to the lordship of Christ through prayer?

GROUP DISCUSSION
1. Spiritual Exercise: Read one book of the Bible for the next 30 days. Read it as many times as you can in one month. Discuss what you learned.

2. When you come into church for a worship service, how can you enter into the worship more fully?

3. What emphasis did Christ place on prayer? (See Matthew 6:9-15; Mark 11:22-25; and John 17.)

Video Resource
John Maxwell—*Becoming a Man of the Word*. To order:
    INJOY MINISTRIES • P.O. Box 7700 • Atlanta, GA 30357
        1-800-333-6506

Music Resource
1. "I Miss My Time With You," by singer Larnell Harris.

2. "Breathe on Me," sung by Susan Ashton, Margaret Becker and Christine Dente on the *Along the Road* CD.

Sources
[1] Frank Hannigan, *Golf Digest*, August 1997, p.71.

[2] "My Eyes Are Dry," by Keith Green on the *No Compromise* album by Sparrow Records, 1978.

Chapter 7

LATITUDE LIVING

Even the longest journey begins with a single step
-16th century adage

For the woman standing on the outer ledge of the State Route 8 bridge, the pain of life's problems and the apparent lack of answers seemed to have made her journey in life no longer worth the effort. From her point of view, the only option was to end it all. All her pain, struggle, and sense of hopelessness would be gone in an instant.

An Akron, Ohio, fire captain, one of the first people on the scene, tried to reason with the woman. He didn't have much success, as she inched closer to the edge. After an hour of negotiations, the woman refused requests to come down or to speak with her son.

That's when Knute Larson, Pastor of The Chapel, got involved. Pastor Larson was in his office when the telephone rang. Apparently, a church member had been driving across the bridge, saw the human drama unfolding, and decided to call Pastor Larson and tell him about it.

"When you hear of something like this, you've got to try and help," Larson says. He jumped into his car and drove to the scene, where he was allowed to speak to the distraught woman. She immediately recognized him from television commercials he had done to inform others about their need for Christ.

"I trust you! I've seen you on T.V.," she told Larson.

He held out his hand, and an hour later the woman took it and climbed back over the rail to safety.

"We talked about our kids and our purpose for being here, about Christ and hope," Larson recalls. "I was praying I could tell her how much she needs to go on living." [1]

If the phone rang in your office, at your home, or when you're just getting ready to go out to the course to tee it up, and someone on the other end of the line was struggling and in great pain in trying to sort out life's circumstances, how would you respond? Would you see it as an unsettling interruption or an opportunity to show to others that what you say is reflected in how you live?

Now, just for a second, let's imagine the person on the other end of the phone is your wife, your child, or a close friend who attends your weekly men's study. They need your help, advice, or a shoulder to cry on. Are you put off by their call or do you respond in the same manner as Christ would?

Our last chapter dealt with how to maintain a proper vertical relationship with God by focusing in on three tacking maneuvers that draw us closer to the Father who loves us. In this chapter we want to examine how that is "fleshed" out in our horizontal relationship with others. How you and I live before others is an excellent barometer of how God is shaping the core of our character.

The depth of our loyalty and intimacy with our Lord is going to be reflected in how we treat those we say we love the most—our family, friends, those within the body of Christ, not to mention those who, with a critical eye, are watching to see if we are truly living out the claims of Christ. Just as a sailor needs to be aware of the atmospheric pressure by reading and studying the barometer, so we must be attentive to the spiritual atmosphere of our homes and church. Do people truly see a difference in our lives because we are navigating our lives by the coordinates of God's Word? In the next two chapters, we'll examine two spiritual barometers that will help us in determining if we are clearly and visibly demonstrating the love and power of God to those around us.

Spiritual Barometer # 1
COMPASSION

The April 22 edition of the *Oklahoman & Times* reported:

In the midst of the horror and chaos wreaked by the deadly bomb blast at the federal building in downtown Oklahoma City, ordinary citizens became heroes. . . Acts of heroism, sacrifice, compassion, and dedication by countless people in the gut-wrenching, agonizing hours in the wake of the dastardly, murderous explosion were so numerous as to be almost commonplace.[2]

Throughout every chapter of our life, we are given a choice. We can become compassionate toward those who need comforted, thus answering the call to be Christ's agents of mercy. Or we can become hard-hearted, insensitive to the emotions and needs of others, thus detaching ourselves from a world that seeks to be held and restored.

In *Requiem for the Heartland*, a photojournalist's book that dedicates its proceeds to the victims of the Oklahoma bombing, one of the photos shows a woman reaching out to another, a stranger who was weeping. "I don't know who you are," she said, "but I know you need a hug."[3]

When compassion becomes a visible barometer to those around, people will feel the freedom to open up and share their hurts, struggles, and pain without fear of judgment or criticism. When a generous outpouring of compassion is exhibited, a safe environment is created where maturity and character is forged.

We don't learn the power of compassion by taking a three hour seminar on the how to's of caring for the downcast and broken-hearted. The best way I have learned to become a compassionate agent in an "I don't want to get involved" culture, is by going "below deck" and spending time with those who are on the edge of hopelessness. It is there that I clearly see the transforming power of Christ's compassion move me, to put hope once again into the heart and soul of a downcast individual.

When He saw the crowds, He had compassion on them, because they were harassed and helpless, like sheep without a shepherd (Matthew 9:36).

Come to Me, all you who are weary and burdened, and I will give you rest. Take My yoke upon you and learn from Me, for I am gentle and humble in heart, and you will find rest for your souls. For My yoke is easy and My burden is light (Matthew 11:28-30).

Karen Mains, author of *Comforting One Another in Life's Sorrows*, says if we are going to display mercy to those who need comforted, "We may have to walk through the sewers of another's life. In the process we may become soiled along the way."[4] We must ask ourselves these questions. Do we want to pay the cost to become comforters to those who are closest to us? Do we want to get involved? To feel their pain? To put hope once again into their darkened situation?

There was a widely published article several years ago about a woman who was brutally raped outside of her apartment complex one evening. For over an hour she pleaded for help and screamed for someone to come to her aid. Later, over 100 people who lived in the apartment complex testified that they had heard the screams and cries for help in the parking lot, but they either did nothing or turned their T.V. volume up to deaden the noise coming from outside. Each person thought the other tenants in the complex would surely call the police and yet nobody did anything. They ignored the situation because they didn't want to get involved.

We need to make sure those in our homes, offices, neighborhoods, and churches who are crying out for help with desperation are not ignored while we grow idle, thinking someone else will come along and fill in the gap.

Compassion is the one quality men have a hard time showing. Not because we don't want to, but because we live in a culture that says, "Don't cry, don't show emotion, suck it up, be a man and go on." It's no surprise, then, that when we are called to demonstrate compassion to another, we become fearful, and our words become awkward. Yet a woman can often come into the same situation, and within seconds, identify, comfort, and wrap her arms around the weakened individual. Why is that? Why do we have such a difficult time expressing comfort to those whom we love the most? There are several reasons.

A LOSS FOR WORDS

Often when placed in a setting or circumstance where compassion needs to be shown to a hurting soul, we are hard pressed to find words or to offer any physical comfort because it seems so foreign to us. What we end up offering are words that provide inadequate comfort for the cry of the weary soul.

Here are just a few of the shallow clichés we offer others when we are struggling ourselves to find words along the way: "Things could be worse." "I'm sorry to hear that." "I'll be praying for you." "Keep the chin up, hang in there, it could be a lot worse." "Fight the good fight and keep running the race." "Press on, brother, God's got his hidden agendas." "Your day is just around the corner." "Wow...what a shame." "There's always tomorrow."

And though all of these sayings may be true, they are often weak substitutes for true biblical compassion. Especially. . .

To the woman who has just learned her husband is having an affair...For the couple who has been called in to the hospital to identify their 16 year old son...For the members of a church who are going through a split...For the brother who is slowly losing his sister to leukemia...For the grieving spouse as they try to keep it together at the grave site of their soul mate.

I have come to realize that the people I most appreciate when life seems to nudge me closer to the edge of despair are not necessarily those who give great advice, ask all the right questions, or even give great answers. I most appreciate the ones who come along and say nothing. That's right, they're great listeners. They know when to talk and when to listen with great concern, just as if Jesus were in their very shoes. Our tenderness will be remembered long after our words will. We would do well to just listen (Proverbs 18:13). "Everyone should be quick to listen, slow to speak" (James 1:19).

NEGLECTING TO GET INVOLVED

Often we don't want to get involved or don't have the time to wade through the struggles and hurt that others are going through. We find quick excuses for avoiding areas where compassion must be expressed. We make statements like, "How can I help them with their pain when there is so much pain and struggle going on in my own life?" Or, "I have a hard enough time carrying my own burdens without having to carry someone else's as well." The fact of the matter is, we are fearful of giving ourselves to someone or something without receiving anything in return.

There are moments while obeying and serving God, where it does seem as though He requires a stripping of pride, prejudices, and reputation on our part, so we can give our all with no holding back, no reservations. It is in this time of personal stripping of self-baggage that we begin to identify and participate in the sufferings of Christ. It is truly in giving that we receive. When our own selfishness is stripped away, it opens the soul to get involved, no matter what the cost.

THE LOST ART OF TOUCHING

When life is shattered, it feels as though there is no framework, no structure, no stability to rest on. For these people life seems dark, hopeless, like a near death experience. For you and me to embrace them, it is literally an expression of Christ's love and compassion being manifested through our lives. Karen Mains shares,

> Touching, or holding, finds expression in a broad range of variables. The fleeting brush of fingers on another's sleeve. The sacramental laying on of hands. The profound steadying that occurs when friends stand strong beside us at our moments of greatest pain. Touch has the power to convey something of God through a very human means.

> Undoubtedly, there are dark moments so desperate that we need someone to come along side us, to climb up into the death bed, as it were, if only figuratively; to hold us tightly, to rock us gently, to protect and cover us so we feel safe to let the grief and anguish rise.[5]

"Modern research reveals that when premature infants are given short daily massages, their growth rate is increased by nearly 50 percent."[6] We too, in many ways, are mere infants. We need others to instill confidence and assurance in us, to cheer us on as we take baby steps towards personal recovery and restoration. As a result, we grow so we may learn to nurse others who, in their "infancy," are too weak to stand on their own.

Life is too short; we are only on this earth for a brief time. Our wives, children, churches and friends need to see a strong man who demonstrates the character of Christ-like compassion in a hardened world. Let us rise up, men of God, and hold tight to those who need to be strengthened.

SEEING COMPASSION AS A SIGN OF WEAKNESS

Compassion is certainly not a trait demonstrated by the weak and feeble. It is a strong masculine trait of godly character. Christ exhibited compassion to those who were sick, diseased, blind, and deaf (Matthew 9:35).

> *So Jesus had compassion and touched their eyes. And immediately their eyes received sight, and they followed Him* (Matthew 20:34).

His display of compassion certainly did not lessen his ministry or His manhood. If anything, it enhanced it. He demonstrated the very essence of His heavenly Father (Hebrews 1:3), by coming to earth to do the will of the Father who sent Him (John 5:19,36; 8:28-30). He humbled Himself and became obedient to death, even death on a cross (Philippians 2:8). Christ knows what it's like to feel pain, sorrow and despair. During His earthly ministry He saw it daily in the eyes of hurting, hopeless people. In doing so, He ministered the agent of compassion on more people than anyone had ever done or will do. We have to conclude, then, that compassion is a key element in ministering to the needs of people all around us. This is seen especially when Jesus entered the Jewish synagogue in Luke 4 and unrolled the scroll of the prophet Isaiah and read Isaiah 61:1-3:

> *The Spirit of the Sovereign Lord is on Me, because the Lord has anointed Me to preach good news to the poor. He has sent Me to bind up the brokenhearted, to proclaim freedom for the captives and release from darkness for the prisoners, to proclaim the year of*

the Lord's favor and the day of vengeance of our God, to comfort all who mourn, and provide for those who grieve in Zion, to bestow on them a crown of beauty instead of ashes, the oil of gladness instead of mourning, and the garment of praise instead of a spirit of despair. They will be called oaks of righteousness, a planting of the Lord for the display of His splendor.

Jim Petersen in his book, *Lifestyle Discipleship*, says,

This is one of the most hope-inspiring passages in the entire Bible. We would do well to commit it to memory. Jesus is saying that the raw materials for His redemptive work are the poor, the heartbroken, and those who are enslaved. He will comfort such people and provide for them. He will exchange their sadness and despair for beauty and praise. He will not just heal them but transform them into "oaks of righteousness." They will be towers of strength and so He will put them to work rebuilding the ruins.[7]

Do you see the power that compassion can play in our role as men? Through compassion we have the privilege of rebuilding ruined lives so that transformation and strength can occur once again. That privilege is given to you and me over and over and over again. Every time we lift the hearts of the hurting we demonstrate the character of Christ, and they have the privilege of seeing the character of Christ in person. There is something very masculine about administering the salve of compassion on those dearest to us.

SHALLOW RELATIONSHIPS

If a man does not sense or see compassion expressed in our life, he will hesitate in sharing his pain, grief, or struggles with us. Safety and security are the two motivating factors for authentic relationships to take place. Many of us have experienced homes, accountability groups, churches, and businesses that are cold and shallow because compassion was the missing link. Marriages, churches, friendships, and parenting suffer as a result. We either become disconnected from others or content with our current relationships, thinking this must be the best it's going to get.

We cannot hold to our breast the broken body of Christ in His church and in this world if we are not willing to become broken ourselves. We are broken people ministering to other broken people. Second Corinthians 1:3-7 is a vivid example of broken people offering comfort to other broken people. This is only made possible because of the comfort we have received from Christ. Relationships become stagnant and superficial when we are unable to go below the surface by relating to another person's pain.

When I begin to see people through the eyes of Christ, I begin giving of myself in a way that brings life once again to the heavy heart of a loved one. Authentic relationships are the mutual exchange of lifting and being lifted. The comforter does more than he or she knows; the one seeking comfort receives more than he or she can understand.

Karen Mains writes, "The church must be a place where we can do spiritual labor within its shelter, a place where our agony is overseen by experts and awaited by concerned friends. The church is a birthing room."[8] The compassion Christ expresses through His people serves as the backbone for warm, authentic relationships.

The local church must be a place where sorrow is turned to joy, trial to triumph, pain to praise. The church must demonstrate authentic compassion. In doing so, we see the resurrection of life occur. The church is a place where we participate in one another's travail and where we share joy and exultation when our work is successfully accomplished. The church must be a place where mercy is given before judgment.

When the church of Jesus Christ visibly demonstrates compassion to those coming in, you will not have to worry about the depth of the people's commitment, but you will have to worry about finding a facility that will be able to shelter everyone.

Take a moment and examine the variety of ways we can show compassion to those who need comfort. These are not in any particular order.

1. Speaking the written Word of God. There are times when a person is drowning in sorrow, and they may not want to hear the Word. Yet

the spoken Word of God is a lifeline that keeps us afloat when the squalls of life seem almost too much to bear.

2.   Reading the written Word of God. The assurance from His Word that God is still working in our life even through the darkest of times can be a cleansing and healing agent of compassion.

3.   Touching them with your hands and arms. We must learn once again the power that a tender touch can have on another. In embracing the cries of the wounded, we do the work of God.

4.   Making eye contact. Sight is extremely important in ministering to individuals. It shows you are interested, your focus is on them, and they are not "just another" project.

5.   Prayer. Pray for the broken person right there and then. This creates a stronger bond of heartfelt concern.

6.   Hearing/Listening. To listen more than speak is a key trait in being an effective compassion agent. One pastor told me, "When a person is bleeding you don't give them a sermon. You help stop the bleeding by taking action." Your tenderness will be remembered long after your words have been forgotten.

7.   Sharing genuine words of encouragement/comfort/affirmation. Think about what you may say that can lift the spirits of an individual.

8.   Take action. Ask, "What can I do to help?" "How can I help ease the pain?" "Children, you show love for others by truly helping them, and not merely by talking about it" (1 John 3:18 cev).

Gordon MacDonald in his book, *When Men Think Private Thoughts,* shares a story of how compassion directly affects the lives of others.

"Friday evening . . . my 8 year old son came to me and asked what cancer was. At this point my Encyclopedia Britannica paid for itself ten times over. I sat him down, read and explained, and asked several times why he wanted to know. He would not tell me. Finally, I closed the book and told him I would not go on until he told me why.

"He then informed me that the friend in his class who had been out for several weeks came back to school, and that he has cancer. He also told me that all the kids made fun of him because he had no hair. He said that he and one of the other boys were trying to be nice to this boy because he was their friend, and that they had decided to do something that would make the other kids stop teasing him.

"When I asked him what they wanted to do, he informed me that they wanted to have their heads shaved so that they looked just like their friend with cancer. I was so touched by my son's show of empathy for a friend. I immediately got on the phone to the other boy's mother. She had just gone through the same conversation with her son.

"Saturday morning we met at the barbershop and had both children's heads shaved. This morning we both got phone calls from the school commending our children for showing such unselfish and caring feelings towards another child, and they were both going to be rewarded for their heroism at the school's last day ceremonies." [9]

Compassion opens up people's hearts like nothing else really can. When shown compassion, we stand amazed, scratching our heads thinking how dynamically different that person is with a simple display of love. Questions flood the mind: What motivated him or her to be so kind? How did he know I needed an act of compassion at my lowest point? Why did she put her own ambitions aside to bring aid and comfort to me? How can I be an agent of compassion for them in the future?

The whole world is going to see God for who He is and will see Jesus for who He is, if Christ's followers show compassion. The power of compassion will turn heads, open hearts, point people to God, and completely change the barometer of your life and others.

⟩⟩ CHARTING YOUR COURSE ⟨⟨

SELF-EVALUATION

1. On a scale of 1 to 10 (1 = barometer falling; 10 = barometer rising) how would you rate your personal compassion for others? Why?

2. When was the last time you wrapped your arms around a hurting soul and cried with them because the pain of life's struggles was almost too much to bear?

3. Meditate on Psalm 62 & 63. Make a mental note of how the Lord seeks to be our refuge, comforter, and strength in time of need. Think of an example of how God has shown these character traits to you.

4. What barriers might keep you from being an agent of compassion to others?

GROUP DISCUSSION
1. Of the five elements expressed, which obstacle do you find difficult to overcome in being an authentic agent of compassion?

2. How has reading this chapter changed your perspective on how you should view, approach, and respond to people who are hurting?

3. As a group, consider taking on the project of sponsoring a child through an organization such as Compassion International. Or maybe you know of someone in your church or neighborhood that needs some groceries, or help around their house. Think of what you can do as a group to show others who are hurting and searching what Christ looks like.

Music Resource:
"Don't Tell Them Jesus Loves Them" by Steve Camp on the *Steve Camp Collection* by Sparrow Corporation. A ballad that challenges us to not just tell someone Jesus loves them, but to demonstrate that love through our actions.

Sources
[1] Getting Out the Word - by Russell D. Sibert - *Akron Beacon Journal* - July 4th, 1993

[2] Oklahoman & Times, April 22, 1995, quoted in *Tides Foundation's Requiem for the Heartland* (San Francisco: Collins Publishers, 1995), p.45.

[3] Requiem for the Heartland

[4] Karen Mains, *Comforting One Another In Life's Sorrows* (Nashville, Tenn. Thomas Nelson Publishers, 1997), p.82.

[5] *Ibid.*, p.71.

[6] Mark Backlin, "Vitamin T: An Extra Dimension of Health," *Prevention* magazine, February 1996, pp. 17-18.

[7] Jim Petersen, *Lifestyle Discipleship* (Colorado Springs, Colorado: NavPress, 1993), p.23.

[8] Karen Mains, *Comforting one Another in Life's Sorrows* (Nashville, Tenn. Thomas Nelson Publishers, 1997), p.187.

[9] Gordon MacDonald, *When Men Think Private Thoughts* (Nashville, Tenn. Thomas Nelson Publishers, 1997), pp. 102-103.

Chapter 8

PASS THE WORD

"If you treat a person as he is, he will remain as he is. If you treat him for what he could be, he will become what he could be."
-Anonymous

When my wife became pregnant with our first child, we were excited like most young couples. We wanted to savor the moment and keep the news to ourselves. Yet, on the other hand, there was that uncontrollable excitement of wanting the world to know that in nine months we would be holding and caring for our own baby. The week my wife and I found out she was pregnant, we decided to tell only our parents and siblings. Then we decided to tell only a few close friends. On Tuesday, I shared it in our staff meeting. By Thursday people were calling our house congratulating us about the great news. When my wife inquired as to how they found out, they said, "So and so told me." What we didn't expect, was on Sunday morning when we arrived at church the dozens upon dozens of people who stopped us in the hall to hug us and tell us how happy they were. I had people hugging me I didn't even know. I wondered how in the world the word got passed so quickly. There was nothing we could do to stop the news. We accepted the fact that for the next nine months everyone we knew would hear and rejoice with us. News travels quickly, doesn't it?

Like a crew on board a ship, the passing of an order, information, or warning is extremely important to the functioning of the ship. The passing of a word can inspire, give hope, create unity and oneness. The failure to pass the word can bring low morale, confusion, and even disaster. Let's examine how we can pass the word of affirmation to those around us, thus creating an atmosphere of unity and usefulness.

Spiritual Barometer # 2
AFFIRMATION

The average person today seeks and craves personal affirmation from others. I believe it is the personal framework of every individual to be loved and appreciated in two distinct ways:

1. *Who we are*—our character and how it is reflected throughout life.

2. *What we do*—the contribution of our gifts, abilities, and efforts.

Studies have shown that, in the average home, for every one positive statement, a child receives ten negative statements. Statements like: "You're not good enough; why can't you be more like..." and "You can't do anything right" cripple our children from functioning effectively. The school environment is only slightly better. Students hear seven negative statements from their teachers for every one positive statement. No wonder so many children grow up feeling that they are losers. Instead of receiving positive affirmation, they have become frustrated and begin to doubt their abilities because of the perception that others have negatively placed on them.

Marlene Wilson, in one of her seminars, shares that people will quit volunteering and serving for a particular task when they are not thanked or affirmed for the contribution and efforts which they are giving to a particular task.

Our homes and churches need to be the two places where we can find genuine affirmation channeled to loved ones. We need a shelter we can go to and hide from a world that seeks to knock us down, beat us up, and remind us around every corner of our personal failures. We need to declare our homes, churches, offices, etc., to be lighthouses of love, direction, affirmation, and encouragement.

How often have you heard from a friend or colleague:
• "We left the church because it seemed cold. No one was putting life into the blood of the Body of believers by encouraging them."

• "I left the company after eight years. I just couldn't handle another day of walking in the office and getting knocked down with critical remarks."

• "Our marriage has been suffering for several years now. It's one sarcastic remark after another from him. I feel like holding up a sign that reads, would somebody please encourage me?"

• "We've made some mistakes along the way with our children. When we should have cheered them on and been proud of them, we discouraged them when we used the word 'but.' Now my children who have grown up and married are doing the same thing to their children."

> *For you know that we dealt with each of you as a father deals with his own children, encouraging, comforting and urging you to live lives worthy of God, who calls you into His kingdom and glory* (1 Thessalonians 2:11-12).

Isn't it great when someone affirms you for who you are or what you've done? Don't you love it when someone in your church, workplace, or family gives you a pat on the back, a kind gesture, or a gift of appreciation for something you've done? I sure do. I live for it. We need it in these tough times in which we live. A simple act of kindness will go miles in fueling the worth and efforts of another in a positive way. But it has to begin with us. True demonstrations of affirmation flow from God's heart to mine and then from my heart to others.

Charles Swindoll in his book, *Growing Wise in Family Life,* expresses how important affirmation and encouragement must first be channeled in our life:

> It is clear that the one who loves himself is better able to love others and relax in their presence. The philosophical framework of all this is rather simple to uncover. Why is it important to love yourself? Because only then are you equipped to love others (Ephesians 5:25). Only then can you bring out the best in the other person (Ephesians 5:27).[1]

When you have a wholesome, confident self-esteem, you're able to love. You're able to give yourself. You're able to pull out what is best in the other person. You're actually able to focus on what is best for them. . . to bring it out, instead of nagging or harassing them."[2]

How can we be a more positive demonstration of Christ's love by fueling others with the power of affirmation?

FUELING YOUR WIFE

Sometimes those in our own families and those whom we love the most are the ones that seem to be the most unappreciated. Displays of affirmation to your wife show her that she is being noticed and useful in contributing to something worthwhile and greater than herself. Affirming your wife lifts her spirit and puts that little bounce back in her step that maybe she needs to get her through the rest of the week.

Affirming your wife also is a sign that you honor her and hold who she is and what she does in high regard. It shows that she is recognized, it enhances her self-esteem, and it gives her a sense of purpose and usefulness.

I try to let my wife know that I appreciate her not just for what she does (and there is certainly a long list), but also for *who she is*. Her generosity, her godly countenance, her patience with our children, etc., are all examples of her character being lived out in the flesh.

You and I can never affirm our wives enough. They deserve it, and they need it. Whether it's the laundry she does just when you're down to your last pair of underwear or the meal she has slaved over all day. Take her in your arms, look directly into her eyes, and thank her, letting her know how much you love her and that you notice all the things she does. Sometimes it's the little things she does to make life a little more enjoyable that especially need to be recognized. Clean sheets, a packed lunch, dropping off the dry cleaning, as well as planning a special night out are all acts of love and kindness.

Take a moment some evening when you're lying in bed and tell your wife three things you appreciate about her. If she faints in the process, that's a good sign you need to be affirming her more.

Or ask the question, "How can I be more of an encouragement to you?" Or buy her a special gift/card. Leave it somewhere where she will find it when you have left for the office, with a note that says, "I notice what you do. I am so blessed. Thank you."

Her children arise and call her blessed; her husband also, and he praises her (Proverbs 31:28).

Just as a boat runs on motor fuel, your wife needs the fuel of affirmation. On a scale from 1-10, how are you doing in giving her the physical, emotional, and spiritual affirmation she needs to function effectively? How full is her tank?

FUELING YOUR CHILDREN

Our children are just as important as our wife. We provide the fuel for their lives. What kind of fuel are we putting into them—positive or negative? Do we set about "catching them doing something good" and then compliment them for it? Or do we pick at what they've done and find the one thing that wasn't done perfectly and comment on it? Are they encouraged or discouraged when we have finished filling up their tank? How far will they be able to go with what we've put in them?

Families who enhance each other's self-esteem are families committed to discovering and understanding one another. Our family consciously works at it. Some days we fail. Other times we accomplish the goal, and the rewards are so satisfying. We're learning to work at finding the good, the strength, the benefit, the hidden counsel, the "plan" in the heart of one another, then drawing it out and valuing it.

A plan in the heart of a man is like deep water, but a man of understanding draws it out (Proverbs 20:5).

Charles Swindoll has some excellent suggestions for family life in his book, *Growing Wise in Family Life*:

Do you have a child who is mechanically inclined? He needs to know you notice. Make comments about it. Brag on his ability. Do you have a child who is athletic, well coordinated? He needs to know you believe he is well coordinated. You say, "That's obvious." But perhaps he hasn't heard it directly from you. He wants to hear you say it. Do you have a child who is intellectually gifted? You sense that she would be good at research, probing deeply into various subjects? Tell her. Mention the future possibilities. Help her find the right university. Rather than hammering away on petty stuff that doesn't matter, spend more time discovering how your children's interest can be channeled. Building a strong self-esteem takes a commitment to discover.[3]

Have you told your children you're proud of them and pointed out a good character trait they've developed rather than a fault? Will your children reach new heights because of what you've instilled into their character?

On a scale from 1-10, how are you doing in giving your children the physical, emotional, and spiritual affirmation they need to function effectively? How full are their tanks?

FUELING YOUR OFFICE

When Dominos Pizza Corporation was just getting on their feet, on one particular day a Domino's Pizza franchise ran out of pizza dough. The president of the corporation, having heard of this, flew to the destination and personally delivered the pizza dough to them and told them to keep up the great work. Now that's affirmation! We need affirmers in our office place. There are too many bitter, frustrated, and ready to throw-in-the-towel employees who need to have their spirits lifted with the fuel of affirmation. An affirmer can change the whole atmosphere of an office setting. When an affirmer walks in, people begin to dream again and the dark cloud of despair is replaced with the sunlight of purpose and laughter. People begin to see through the petty problems and begin to communicate with words that build and bond. People begin to listen and take note once again of others efforts, all because one person determined in his heart that he was not going to cave in to the atmosphere of criticism and backbiting.

Being the affirmer in your office place will change the atmosphere in two ways:

1. They will see a true picture of the character of Christ demonstrated through words of encouragement and appreciation (Ephesians 4:29).

2. It enables others to follow the example by affirming someone else.

As like attracts like, they will find themselves affirming others because they see the value and importance it had to them in their life (1 Thessalonians 1:3).

David Yonggi Cho, pastor of the famous Yoido Full Gospel Church in Seoul, Korea—the world's largest, with some 750,000 members—has an interesting rule for his congregation: "No witnessing to your neighbor until after three good deeds." The Christians there are actually forbidden to mention the name of Jesus to someone until they have first helped that person fix an appliance, have brought in a meal during sickness, or have shown some other kindness. Cho believes that only after three such acts will the heart be open to the Gospel.[4]

We would do well to follow the same steps in our office. May we demonstrate the love of Christ to others by doing deeds that will affirm them and build them up. In the end they will be more open to hearing about the Gospel of Christ because they have seen it lived out. Let's be reminded of the words of Christ in Matthew 5:16. "In the same way, let your light shine before men, that they may see your good deeds and praise your Father in heaven."

On a scale from 1-10, how are you doing in giving those in your office the physical, emotional, and spiritual affirmation they need to function effectively? How full are their tanks?

FUELING YOUR CHURCH

"I quit, I give up. People could care less whether I serve in this area." Do those words sound familiar? Maybe they have come out of your mouth, or you overheard it from a member at your church. Either way, it brings a chill with it, that someone is unhappy, unappreciated, and is willing to walk away from using their gifts or abilities because they haven't been noticed. It's easy to call them selfish. After all they're not working for man, but for God. They should not be looking for acknowledgment or an opportunity to be noticed. I realize that. But too many times those within the Body of Christ are taken advantage of far more than they are affirmed. A simple kind word or gesture acknowledging their contribution to the Body of Christ is always welcomed like a warm blanket. Often, it's the faithful few who are doing the majority of the work while the other saints in the church are benefitting from their efforts.

God has placed us in the Body of believers to serve and to affirm. Being an affirmer in your church creates an atmosphere that leads others to recognize and use their gifts, talents, and efforts on a regular basis. It reminds us that the gifts He has bestowed on us give us the ability and privilege to serve the Body more effectively. Being affirmed reminds us it is Christ working in us and through us. He ultimately gets the glory because without the use of His gifts in our life, we would have very little to offer to others. Our efforts and responsibilities, no matter how big or small, help us see that they are never wasted in God's eyes. Here are a few suggestions of how we can build up those within the Body of Christ.

1. Take them out to lunch and pick up the check.

2. Buy a special gift that signifies how much you appreciate them.

3. Send a card. Always write positives; never write negatives. Form letters don't cut it. They are cold and impersonal. Memos are even worse.

4. Have them over to your house for dinner.

5. Send a thank-you note to the nursery workers or Sunday school teachers who are making an impact on your children while you are in the worship service.

6. As a parent of a teen, call your youth pastor and have him over for dinner to show your gratitude for all he does.

7. Help organize a banquet of appreciation for those who faithfully serve in different areas. Have a banner that says, You Are Noticed!

When affirmation is expressed in the church, you will see people smile more, laugh more, and elect themselves for various tasks, because they see how they are a contributor to the whole picture of community.

On a scale from 1-10, how are you doing in giving those in your church the physical, emotional, and spiritual affirmation they need to function effectively? How full are their tanks?

Why might the spiritual atmosphere in your church, marriage, or relationships be steadily dropping on the affirmation barometer? Here are three possible reasons:

1. *Plagued by personal crises.* We often don't show appreciation to others because it's the last thing on our minds. Stress, struggles, and schedules are pushed to the forefront of our thinking, making it difficult to express our gratitude and appreciation to others. We have become so distracted in our fast-paced culture that we have forgotten what a single act of affirmation can do for the life and countenance of another person.

We have become so engrossed in our own self-interests that we forget to look to the interests of others (Philippians 2:1-5). When affirmation is demonstrated to an individual, it instills confidence and reassurance that they are important and what they do is important.

2. *Few oases in the desert.* The times when we receive or give personal affirmation to another are usually few and far between in those desert experiences. We will go days, weeks, even months when no one says a word. We wonder if anyone really cares or knows the effort we are putting forth. We must create more opportunities, more oases in peoples lives. If we don't, it will breed stagnation and a state of vegetation in our relationships.

3. *False assumption.* We assume that someone else is carrying the load of affirming others. The problem may be that they are assuming you are carrying the load. NEVER ASSUME. If we are going to assume anything, then assume that no one has been told or shown that they are important and their skills are valuable to the health of the team. Then go and do it.

> *Let us not grow weary in doing good, for at the proper time we will reap a harvest if we do not give up. Therefore, as we have opportunity, let us do good to all people, especially to those who belong to the family of believers* (Galatians 6:9-10).

Our words have power (Proverbs 11:25; 18:21). They can be words of life when used to benefit and lift the soul of an individual. They can also deliver a death blow that can wound and leave scars for years to come. Let's offer words of life. "To life!" shout the dancers and actors in the musical *Fiddler on the Roof*. It is when we channel affirmation into the life of others that they will shout with laughter and joy, "To life!"

CHARTING YOUR COURSE

SELF-EVALUATION

1. In what one area mentioned could you do a better job of fueling someone through affirmation?

2. How will demonstrating affirmation help in developing Christ-like character in your life? (See Romans 15:4-7; Philippians 2:1-5; Hebrews 3:13; and 10:24-25.)

3. Sometime this week, affirm a close friend by sharing three qualities you admire in them.

4. How can you be more of an encouragement to your closest friends?

GROUP DISCUSSION

1. Take some time in your group for each person to affirm something about either his wife or someone in the group, for who he/she is or does.

2. Discuss: How strong is your church in affirming one another within the Body of Christ? How could this be improved?

Sources
[1] Charles Swindoll, *Growing Wise in Family Life*, Portland, Oregon: Multnomah Press, 1988 p.141.

[2] *Ibid.*, p.139.

[3] *Ibid.*, p. 141.

[4] *Dean Merrill, Sinners in the Hands of an Angry Church*, Grand Rapids, Michigan: Zondervan Publishing House, 1997, pp.65-66.

COORDINATE #3

Navigating
Our Time and Priorities

Chapter 9

MAN OVERBOARD

*"Any fool can carry on but a wise man knows
how to shorten sail in time."* —Unknown

The USS America Aircraft Carrier is a floating city, with a crew of more than 4600 and with 79 aircraft. It is November 29, 1995, as the giant vessel cuts its way through the cold black Arabian sea, moving into position to support U.S. troops in Bosnia.

Lance Corporal Zachary Mayo is stationed on the USS America. He cannot sleep. It's two in the morning. He rises from his bed and goes outside for a breath of fresh air. He steps out onto the pilot's platform (a narrow deck 30 feet above the swirling ocean water.) Suddenly the ship changes course, causing a door directly behind him to fly open, sending him sailing into the waters below. Instantly Mayo slides from one end of the food chain to the other. Disoriented, he finally finds his way to the surface. Mayo begins yelling and screaming, hoping someone on the back of the ship will see him or hear him. No one does. Mayo watches in horror as the vessel sails away into the night. There would be no swimming to shore for Zachary Mayo. He is some 200 miles off the Pakistani coast. He's alone and afraid. He's treading water, and no one even knows he's missing.

It is now some 24 hours later, and Mayo is still treading water. "Water, water everywhere but not a drop to drink." No way to signal for help, and no life jacket. "Being a Marine we are taught over and over again to keep going, and to never quit," says Mayo. Mayo didn't quit and literally survived by the seat of his pants. "I took my overalls off and tied the legs into knots. I inflated them with air by taking them over my head and throwing air into them. That served as a makeshift life preserver. The only problem with that was the air leaked out every couple of minutes so I had to do this maneuver again and again. I'm sure I did this maneuver at least 1000 times."

It is now 36 hours since Mayo went overboard. His tongue begins to swell due to lack of water. He begins to hallucinate; he is tired and sleepy. He knows if he stops treading water, he's finished. "I began to think about my family and God, something I had not done in quite a while."

Hours later the sea began to turn rough, and the waves got higher. Mayo's head was burned from the all day sun and his body chilled to the bone at night after the sun had disappeared on the horizon. "I just held on to the hope that someone was going to find me and rescue me. Yet no one came. I began to wonder how long I could hold out."

In dire thirst, physically exhausted, and treading water in his sleep, Mayo awoke in the morning, not to the sight of a ship approaching, but to the sight of hungry sharks. He was entering into shark infested waters, but ironically that may be what saved his life. A Pakistani fishing boat was hunting for sharks, but instead they found Zachary Mayo, naked, delirious, but alive. When Mayo was found he had been treading water for over three days. "It was the greatest thing," said Mayo, "to be able to put my feet on land again, on solid ground."[1]

HOW LONG CAN YOU TREAD WATER?

Have you felt swept overboard by life's sudden change of course, or caught off guard by the swinging door of schedules, deadlines, confrontations, and relationship pressures? Have you found yourself treading through the pressures of work, finances, family situations, not to mention trying to find time for your personal walk with Christ? How often do we find ourselves either thinking about or verbalizing over the agonizing pressure of being under the pile of things rather than on top of them? I sure have made these statements from time to time, have you?

The reality for many of us is that we live in a whirlwind culture where everyone and everything demands our time and attention. We are overwhelmed, overloaded, and in dire need of an overhaul. If we don't begin to manage our time and priorities better, we will be led about by our nose, by circumstances, or by people who will think and plan our life for us.

Currently, what are the distress signals that you see in yourself and in others that indicates a need to be helped and pulled to shore before giving up or giving in? I wonder if you can relate to the distress signals that appear on the very hull of our hearts from time to time:

DELTA: "Keep clear of me, I'm maneuvering with difficulty."
BRAVO: "I'm taking in water."
VICTOR: "I require assistance."
MIKE: "My vessel is stopped and making no way through the water."
YANKEE: "I'm dragging anchor."
ZULU: "I require a tug."

Now check out the signals that Jesus Christ seeks to tie to the mast of our vessel, not just for today or tomorrow, but for the rest of our days:

QUEBEC: "My vessel is healthy, and I request free clearance."
KILO: "I wish to communicate with you."
X-RAY: "Stop carrying out your intention and watch for my signals."[2]

MOSES TREADING WATER

Let's take a look at the life of Moses and see how God used another individual to come to Moses' aid and provide guidance and strength when he was wondering, "How long can I tread water without going under?"

When Israel was camped in the desert near Mount Sinai, Jethro (Moses' father-in-law) sent Moses this message: "I am coming to visit you, and I am bringing your wife and two sons."

When they arrived, Moses went out and bowed down in front of Jethro, then kissed him. After they had greeted each other, they went into the tent, where Moses told him everything the Lord had done to protect Israel against the Egyptians and their king. He

*also told him how the Lord had helped them in all their troubles.
Jethro was so pleased to hear this good news about what the Lord
had done that he shouted, "Praise the Lord! He rescued you and
the Israelites from the Egyptians and their king. Now I know that
the Lord is the greatest God, because He has rescued Israel from
their arrogant enemies." Jethro offered sacrifices to God. Then
Aaron and Israel's leaders came to eat with Jethro there at the
place of worship* (Exodus 18:6-12 cev).

What a celebration! Moses is overwhelmed about all that God has
done. His enthusiasm gets Jethro excited, which causes great rejoicing
among the people. It seems as if things couldn't be better. God is
faithful, and He has shown His goodness to His people by rescuing
them from the wicked schemes of Pharaoh and out of the hardships of
the Egyptians. God truly has directed His people to solid ground.
Even though there was pain, grief, and trials along the way, the people
now recognize that God intended it for their good and for the glory of
His name.

In verse nine, Jethro is so delighted to hear about all the good
things the Lord has done for Israel that He shouts, "Praise the Lord!"
God's mighty power has been shown throughout the nations. In response to God's goodness, a sacrifice offered in praise and adoration is
lifted up to God, causing it to be a sweet smelling aroma in His nos-
trils (see Numbers 15:3; 2 Corinthians 2:15).

Maybe you're reading this and you're saying, "So what? What does
that have to do with my current situation?" It has great significance to
your situation. When we can identify where God has shown to us His
goodness and power in the past, we can be certain that His goodness
and faithfulness will be evident and confirmed in our life once again in
a transforming way.

Compare your situation to that of Moses and His people. God's
hand was on Moses' shoulder during times of celebration as well as in
times of treading water. When we feel like we've been thrown overboard, remember the sacrifice of praise that has come from our lips in
the past and how God provides a way, comes to our rescue, and will
see us through. His heart's desire is not to see us cast overboard,
struggling to stay above the water, but to pull us in and set our feet

once again on the solid rock of His Son Jesus Christ. Let's keep this verse fresh on our minds, or should I say lips:

Through Jesus, therefore let us continually offer to God a sacrifice of praise—the fruit of lips that confess His name. And do not forget to do good and to share with others, for with such sacrifices God is pleased (Hebrews 13:15-16 NIV).

As well as things are going for Moses, it's only a matter of time before the clouds move in and the squalls of life begin to beat at the hull of his vessel. In verses 13-16, the people are beginning to overload Moses with a cargo of concerns, complaints, and criticisms:

The next morning Moses sat down at the place where he decided legal cases for the people, and everyone crowded around him until evening. Jethro saw how much Moses had to do for the people, and he asked, "Why are you the only judge? Why do you let these people crowd around you from morning till evening?" Moses answered, "Because they come here to find out what God wants them to do. They bring their complaints to me, and I make decisions on the basis of God's laws" (CEV).

I can just hear Moses saying, "Last night was a night to remember; it's almost to good too be true." And in this case it really was. The very next morning after a joyous evening of worship and sacrifice, Moses is bombarded by the immediate affairs of the people. He doesn't even get to reflect on all that went on the night before. Back to the rat race of life. Sound familiar? For Moses, it's ongoing from morning till evening. Never a second to get up, stretch, and take in the serene sunset on the horizon. Do you know why? Because it's obstructed by thousands of people wanting their case dealt with, and dealt with NOW!

Well that's his job, that's his calling, you might be thinking. No, it's not! Moses was not called by God, and neither are we, to be a full-time fire fighter. Constantly putting out small fires for others throughout the week leaves your emotional, physical, and spiritual tanks drained when you go home or when you walk through the front doors of your local church. Is it a responsibility for Moses? Yes. But Moses needs a life as well. He needs some time to get a breath of fresh air and a clearer perspective on life. If Moses continues to sit there day after day, trying to handle the disputes that are brought to his attention, he will inevitably become hard and cynical.

We cannot expose ourselves to the sinful nature of others' complaints and criticisms without it having some kind of effect on us as well. It is Jethro who recognizes Moses' need for help. Notice that Jethro doesn't tell Moses to wash his hands of this whole clan of people and go back to shepherding, but he asks Moses a very perceptive question. "Why do you ALONE sit as judge?" In other words, where is your help? When your back is up against the wall and you need some comrades to come along and provide strength and wisdom, who do you turn to?

We would do well to ask the same. Where are the people you trust, that you can lean on, who will help ease the load you bear? We will grow weary when we try to do it alone, and this will often result in emotional, physical, and spiritual burnout. If we think we can save the company, the church, or even our family by being the sole burden bearer, we will become drained in the process. Jethro was more than just a father-in-law, he was a wise friend who was honest enough to level with Moses about his current condition. Moses would probably have gone to an early grave due to the overload of stress had Jethro not brought this to his attention.

Moses' response to Jethro in verse 15 is valid. "The people come to me to seek God's will." Jethro is not questioning Moses' intent, but the way he is going about it. He is going about it *alone*, a sure way to ruin a good leader whom people are leaning on. He is surrounded by sharks which, in time, will begin to take bite sized chunks out of his vessel. You and I cannot make clear decisions during times of spiritual and emotional weariness. Weariness, anxiety, and stress become prominent factors when busyness takes the place of relationship building. When the load in ministry, marriage, or work is not adequately shared, the people doing the majority of the work will eventually become under attack and spiritually undernourished. If the enemy cannot get you to do something wrong, he will get you to do something busy.

Richard Swenson, M.D., in his book, *Margin*, has done extensive research on the subject of those who are overloaded and have extended themselves too thin.

"Margin," says Swenson "is the leeway we once had between ourselves and our limits. It is the extra space between the things we must do and our capacity. When we use up all of that space, we are working at full capacity and there is no margin left. Then, when extra demands come or something unexpected arises, we suffer overload. We feel harassed, suffer stress, and experience all sorts of negative effects on our health and our emotions."

As a medical doctor, Swenson found himself attending a parade of patients whose basic problem was really overload. He concludes, "Something is wrong. People are tired and frazzled. People are anxious and depressed. People don't have time to heal anymore." Swenson enumerates a long list of overloads that causes us pain. We can be overloaded with activities, with choices, commitments, debts, education, expectations, fatigue, information, media, ministry, people, work, traffic, and on and on. Chronically overloaded people lose their capacity to respond. Often they are misunderstood as being weak, apathetic, or lacking in commitment."[3]

In 1880, Samuel Plimsoll of the United Kingdom tackled the problem of having overloaded vessels sink in heavy seas. He submitted a bill in Parliament insisting that a line be drawn around the outside of the hull on all British ships. When the ships were loaded with freight and reached the level where the line hit the water, the ships were not allowed to load anymore. In turn, they would find another vessel's hull that wasn't as full going to the same destination so they might use it without overloading any one vessel. The marking on the ships hull became known as the Plimsoll line.[4] Where's your Plimsoll line today? Some of us are overloaded and at risk of sinking. We can lighten the load of another brother or sister in Christ by taking on some of their responsibilities.

Two are better than one, because they have a good return for their work: if one falls down his friend can help him up. But pity the man who falls and has no one to help him up!" (Ecclesiastes 4:9-10)

THE GREAT ALBATROSS

For ages sailors have considered it bad luck to harm the far ranging sea bird, the albatross. The albatross was immortalized by Coleridge in his "Rime of the Ancient Mariner," and many say it was this poem that made the superstition so popular. Contrary to this theory, however, it has been said that the assistant navigator on board the ill-fated Titanic was named Albert Ross, whom it was rumored was very bad luck to have around. For decades after the sinking of the Titanic, old sailors could be heard to say things like, "It must have been an Albert-Ross," when discussing the fate of a missing ship. Thus the confusion arose with the sea bird.[5]

I think Moses felt like he had an albatross tied around his neck while wading through the burdens of the people of Israel. Jethro decided to help take the heaviness of this albatross off the shoulders of Moses by offering him some godly wisdom like only a father-in-law can.

"What you are doing is not good...you will only wear yourself out" (Exodus 18:17-18). Jethro sees his son-in-law on the brink of exhaustion and in dire need of an overhaul. Does that sound like you? Like a rubber band stretched to the point of snapping? You take on too much, you can't say no, and you handle (or at least try to) the demands alone? Moses was smart to listen to Jethro. He was hearing the advice of a wise man who saw Moses' situation from a different angle. Moses had to determine, as we should, which things he had to handle himself (the much more difficult issues) and what to pass on to others.

SHIFTING THE LOAD

How is Moses going to handle this delicate task of shifting some of the load to those within the camp? Through the advice of Jethro, Moses decided to select faithful and God-fearing individuals to balance the work load that confronted him.

> *You will need to appoint some competent leaders who respect God and are trustworthy and honest. Then put them over groups of ten, fifty, a hundred, and a thousand. These judges can handle the ordinary cases and bring the more difficult ones to you. Having them share the load will make your work easier. This is the way God wants it done. You won't be under nearly as much stress, and everyone else will return home feeling satisfied* (Exodus 18:21-23).

Take a look at the kind of qualities Jethro told Moses to look for in finding good help and leadership. Ask yourself if you have people in and around your life with the same qualities. It's imperative, as we delegate responsibility to others, that we know and believe in the people to whom we are delegating. On several occasions I put the wrong man in a certain position only for it to result in disaster. Observe the people to whom you seek to delegate responsibility. Be careful that you don't end up regretting a rash decision because you wanted a problem off your desk or off your mind ASAP. Moses chose the right people. The albatross was lifted, order was regained, and he could stretch and gaze at that breathtaking sunset at the end of the day.

We dream of calm seas and steady gentle winds, where days are warm and clear. What we end up getting hit with in the forecast of life, however, is quite different. How can we practically begin to avoid or deal with those unexpected overboard situations that come without warning? How can we navigate our priorities and schedules so we can enjoy life and not despise it? Let me throw you five life preservers to hang onto.

1. *Define the problem.* What continues to be an albatross around your neck that weighs you down? Identify it.

2. *Determine the plan.* What damage has it done or is it doing that is affecting your soul, family, friends, and walk with the Lord?

3. *Decide on the proper course of action.* When Jonah and the other sailors on the ship headed towards Joppa and sailed into a violent storm, they had to decide in a matter of seconds what cargo needed to be thrown overboard (Jonah 1:1-16). God is asking you and me today, as we strive to navigate our lives towards biblical manhood, what needs to be thrown overboard so that it will not hinder us from the journey Christ has mapped out for us.

4. *Draw on God's perfect strength.* We can either focus our eyes on the one in the crow's nest, the author and perfecter of our faith, Jesus Christ (Hebrews 12:2), or we can set our gaze on the pile of life's pain, pressure, and potential problems before us. God promises He will provide strength for the weary and increase the power of the weak.

As our hope and perspective is on Him, He will renew our strength so we can soar like eagles (Isaiah 40:29-31).

Take a moment and pray this great hymn of faith as you draw on His strength:

"Leave it there.....leave it there.....take your burden to the Lord and leave it there.....if you trust and never doubt, He will surely bring you out; take your burden to the Lord and leave it there."[6]

5. *Delegate to others.* Begin to give faithful and responsible people some of the load you carry around. I heard somewhere that if we could kick the person responsible for most of our problems, most of us wouldn't be able to sit for weeks. Stop thinking that if you delegate responsibility to others that in some way that makes you weak. It's not a sign of weakness; it's a sign of humility. We rob ourselves of an opportunity to experience life to the fullest when we arrogantly neglect to delegate. We also rob the individual who is capable of handling the task of an opportunity to use his or her gifts, talents, and energies in a new and stretching way.

CHARTING YOUR COURSE

SELF-EVALUATION

1. "Margin," says Swenson, "is the leeway or time we once had between ourselves and our limits." How much margin do you give yourself between events or circumstances to: Think? Heal? Rest? Play? How can a proper "margin" be maintained for a healthier outlook on life?

2. Like Jethro's challenge to Moses (see Exodus 18), who are the people you can begin to delegate responsibility to, so you might free yourself up in doing the most important areas?

3. After reading the account of Moses and Jethro in Exodus 18, what steps can you take to keep yourself from becoming overloaded?

4. What will be the benefit of sharing your stress with a wise counsel of friends (see Proverbs 15:22) when you are on the verge of: spiritual, physical, or emotional overload?

5. Is it hard for you to delegate responsibility to others? Why?

6. Exercise: What four things/areas are pressing you right now? Write them down on a 3x5 card and put them away for six months and then come back to it and see where you are at with them by asking:

A. What has changed in six months?

B. When I see these areas of concern, are they still a concern?

C. Have any of these areas been solved due to delegation?

D. Do I look at these areas and wonder why I was so stressed out?

GROUP DISCUSSION

1. How do the following verses encourage you in establishing correct priorities and personal time management? (Ecclesiastes 3:1-8; 4:6,9-12; 10:10; 12:13-14)

Music Resource: "Busy Man" by Billy Ray Cyrus, *Shot Full of Love.*

Video Resource: *Margin* by Richard Swenson M.D. can be purchased through: Dallas Christian Video, 1878 Firman, Richardson, Texas 75081, (972) 644-1905.

Sources

[1] Dateline NBC, Burrelle's Transcripts, *Dateline Survivor: Man Overboard*, June 12th, 1996 Livingston, New Jersey.

[2] Joachim Schult, *The Sailing Dictionary,* (Sheridan House, Dobbs Ferry, New York, 1992), pp.332-333.

[3] Richard Swenson, M.D., *Margin,* (Colorado Springs, Co: NavPress, 1992), pp.83-87.

[4] Hyrum W. Smith, *The 10 Natural Laws of Successful Time and Life Management,* (Warner Books, New York, New York, 1994), p.37.

[5] Chris Hillier, *The Devil and The Deep,* (Sheridan House, Dobbs Ferry, New Jersey, 1997) p.1.

[6] "Leave It There," Arr. by Charles A. Tindley, Jr., *Tabernacle Hymns,* (Tabernacle Publishing Co., Chicago, Illinois), pp.223-224.

Chapter 10

SAGGING SAILS AND CREAKY JOINTS

Make your life and body a priority!
–Stephen Arterburn, M.Ed.

I had to laugh out loud! The friend I was talking with was a portly man to put it modestly, but when he said, "I always watch my waist-line—I've got it out in front where I can keep my eye on it," I couldn't hold it back. We both had a good laugh, and then he turned and admitted, "If I don't lose some weight it's going to kill me." *That,* I thought, *isn't something to laugh about, my friend.*

We have already addressed the reality that we are often over-whelmed, overloaded, and in dire need of a spiritual overhaul. Yet there are many of us who are overweight, and if we don't begin to take better care of ourselves it may result in a trip to the pine box!

Remember your high school reunions? They have a way of calling to our attention that we're not getting any younger. There's more sand in the bottom of the hour glass than on top. Our thoughts when attending our first five year reunion may go something like this:

"I'm going to go because I want to see how some of my friends are doing." Job market, financial security, and marriage are the big conversation. Children's pictures are strategically laid out with great satisfaction and intent so that all may see and comment.

The 10 year reunion is the eye opener. Our thoughts may be: "I have hardly changed at all, but I want to see how others have changed." As we enter the room, we are confronted with people who have widened and expanded their dress and belt sizes a few notches. That knockout dreamboat now looks more like a tug boat. And that high school prom king that the girls practically fainted over when he walked by has certainly changed. His abs have turned to flabs, and this hunk is now a chunk. As we drive home with a dose of reality of the physical changes we see in others, we look at our own bodies and think, "Have I, too, in some way let my body go to the extent that it gives the evidence of lack of exercise and self-discipline?"

The 20–30 year reunions are usually the best. There is a sea of gray hair as you walk through the doors. Pictures are pulled out immediately in order to brag about grandchildren. There is not a sense of one-upmanship, but there is a definite sense that everyone has changed. Several chapters have come and gone since those high school days. We speak more on the memories of the past than the affairs of the present.

How's the vessel of your life holding up on the outside? Are the sails beginning to sag, are the joints beginning to creak? I know talking about exercising, losing weight, and keeping personal disciplines in check can be a sensitive issue for some people. Some excellent books have been written on this subject of dietary and personal upkeep of the body. My intention is not to compete with them, but I do believe that it's just as important to take care of our physical bodies as it is to deal with the onslaught of personal and internal situations occurring in our lives. If we're going to maintain proper coordinates toward biblical manhood, then we must be in tune with the personal maintenance program for our bodies in navigating our lives.

Many have come close to dancing with death due to ignoring important aspects about weight, annual check-ups, personal exercise, and adequate rest. It's usually when we have had a good scare that we finally do something about it. Men who are overweight can develop unnecessary ulcers, heart problems, fatigue, and severe back pain. When we fail to exercise, rest adequately, or shed those pounds that we have been talking about losing for years, it will eventually drain the inner spirit. The result can be that we become lethargic and passive about things that at one time charged our spiritual, emotional, and relational tanks.

Every year I take a group of men from our church for a three-day get away into Pennsylvania for a time of spiritual and relational building. Over those three days, we go white water rafting and back-packing. Months prior to our trip, I inform the men that they need to get out and walk, exercise, and try to lose some weight they may have put on during the winter months. "You don't need to be in great shape for this," I tell them, "but you do need to loosen up the joints and tuck in those sagging waistlines if you want to enjoy our time to-gether." It never fails that during the first day of backpacking we will usually have one or two men who have obviously ignored the prepara-tion exercise. Gasping for air as they walk up an upgrade that goes from a 1,000 foot elevation to over 2,000 in just under one mile, I hear comments like, "I need to lose some weight. I'm out of shape. I haven't exercised like this in years." In the end, we do have a great time. Everyone makes it, but it's also a great eye opener for those who realize that sometimes it's not only the spiritual and relational side that needs to be addressed, but the physical as well.

Stephen Arterburn in his book, *Gentle Eating*, gives some excellent insight into our personal attitudes toward exercising:

> I told myself a lot of reasons that I could not exercise. I put hundreds of barriers between me and the act of getting my body moving. When I broke through all the excuses and started to move and breathe, I felt I had accomplished some-thing spectacular. That good feeling and attitude boosted my self-confidence and motivated me to do more and more for myself and future.

> Gentle, gradual increases in exercise burn off the fat. Go too fast and you will crash and burn. If you can ease into your pro-gram, never getting tired or too sore, you will have a greater chance of continuing to increase your fitness level. It won't happen quickly. But once you begin, you won't turn back. You will wonder why you waited so long to get moving.[1]

Take a moment to honestly answer this humorous physical ques-tionnaire on the current upkeep of your body. If you answer yes to five or more of these, then it's time to seek some help on how you can get into better shape or lose some pounds which might be weighing you down.

1. Was getting out of bed this morning the last time you stretched your muscles and did a sit up?

2. Do you have a club membership, but haven't been there for weeks?

3. Do you break into a sweat walking to the refrigerator or mail box?

4. Do most of your health problems occur due to being overweight and eating at too many greasy spoon restaurants?

5. Does the scale in your home try to hide when it sees you coming?

6. Are you still telling your friends you need to take a few pounds off, yet you realize that words are cheap if not backed by actions?

7. Are the airplane and movie theater seats getting a little tight?

8. Do you keep putting off that regular check up at the doctors out of fear of what they might tell you, or out of embarrassment?

9. Has your waist size exceeded your inseam over the years?

10. Is your idea of a diet only one bag of chips instead of two?

GETTING DOWN TO THE ROOT PROBLEM

For some of us it's not the weight or the lack of energy we have in getting off the couch and strapping on the running shoes that is the root problem. Often the problem is much deeper. Depression can play a big part in developing unhealthy habits. Situations, conflicts, even strained relationships can set an individual on a detour of harmful binges (one of which is food). We eat to numb the pain we are feeling. Circumstances in life which we cannot deal with or are out of our control will often cause us to bury our troubles by suppressing them with food.

"One problem area can control other areas of your life. A negative attitude about food affects relationships, work, or school. But when you start to change one area, the other areas are affected, also. That is why I recommend that if people are struggling with their weight, they should also be working on the other problem areas of their lives at the same time. How do you view your relationships? How do you view God? How do you view your purpose in life? Think of these things. Allow yourself to re-create attitudes in all areas, not just food. As you do, you will find that the battles with food attitudes will be much easier."[2]

Let's be reminded that we are a representative of Jesus Christ. For the temple of God resides within us (1 Corinthians 6:19-20). Proper physical upkeep is important not only for our health, but it also shows that we are living out the disciplines which God has laid down in His Word. For we are an image bearer of God. Let's stay in shape so we are fit for the Lord's work.

So whether you eat or drink or whatever you do,
do it all for the glory of God (1 Corinthians 10:31).

 CHARTING YOUR COURSE

SELF-EVALUATION

1. What attitudes have you developed towards personal discipline of your body? Are these attitudes healthy or unhealthy?

2. What benefits do you gain in getting adequate rest and exercise? (See 1 Timothy 4:8.)

3. What temporary "binges" do we use to numb the pain from life's situations, conflicts, or strained relationships?

4. What is a possible plan of action for becoming more "shipshape"?

GROUP DISCUSSION

1. What excuses do you use to avoid working on the physical upkeep of your body? Are these excuses ever legitimate?

2. What do you think of the statement, "A loss of control in our eating or lack of exercise is an extension of other areas that are out of alignment as well"? Agree or Disagree?

Sources
1. Stephen Arterburn, *Gentle Eating* (Nashville, Tenn.: Thomas Nelson Publishers, 1994), pp.43-44.

2. *Ibid.*, p.49.

COORDINATE #4

Navigating
Toward
Wholesome Thinking

Chapter 11
SWAB THEM DECKS, MATE!

May I think my thoughts after Thee, O God.

Steve (that's not his real name) lingered around as one of our Men's Ministry meetings was letting out. I could tell from his countenance that something heavy was on his heart. Sooner or later he was going to have to lower the boom and share it. We stood and talked for several minutes. Finally I said, "So, what's on your mind, Steve?"

Steve took a deep breath and replied, "I'm almost embarrassed to say, but I'm really struggling with some things right now in my life."

I didn't pry, but I listened as he shared about work, his walk with Christ, family, priorities, etc. I listened as he danced around the "real issue" he was longing to bring to the surface and discuss.

Finally, I thought, *Okay, let's stop dancing and get to the heart of your need.* "Steve, let me ask you a question." It's a question that I have probably asked 95% of the men who attend our meetings on a weekly basis. "What is the biggest area you struggle with as a man of God?"

That question almost inevitably pinpoints the problem. Most of the time the answers are a toss up between finding time for God, dealing with their thought life, or controlling their lustful passions. Steve looked at me, and with all the cards on the table, unloaded what he had been trying to suppress and keep down for years.

"Pornography," said Steve. "I have never told anyone that in my life, but after what you shared tonight about preparing our minds for action (1 Peter 1:13-16), I knew it was time to recognize my problem with pornography and come clean and get some help so I can truly begin to think as Jesus thinks."

We spent a good amount of time over the next few weeks discussing his cry to get out from under the pile of pornography. Steve is not alone. There are thousands of other men in our nation just like Steve who have drifted from wholesome thinking and living.

As I walked with Steve to his car that evening, I will never forget his parting words to me. "Images which have been etched in my mind for years can be brought up with such clarity and unbelievable detail that it scares me. Yet I can read a passage of Scripture 5,000 times and still struggle in memorizing and recalling it for any length of time."

"That's me! That's where I'm at right now," you might say. You are right in the heat of the battle with your back against the wall, and you don't know what to do or who to call on. The cry for help may be different for you than it is for Steve, but the cry of wanting to find a way to strategically prepare our minds to be thinking and focusing on things above rather than on the things of this world (Colossians 3:1-2) is a vitally important one.

The swabbing of the decks of our minds has got to be done on a divine level, not by human willpower. As strong and confident as we think we are in battling with the mind and disciplining our thoughts, we, like Steve, find ourselves struggling with ambitions, desires, and dreams that can sabotage a man's character. On more than one occasion, we have found ourselves being conquered by unwholesome thoughts rather than conquering them. In desperation and frustration, we throw our arms up in disgust. We have more questions than we do answers as to why our thoughts so quickly ping pong back and forth from godly thoughts and intentions to depraved and selfish ambitions. No doubt, it's getting tougher every day to think and live a life of holy character. From television, to the newsstand, to the Internet, today's Christian is constantly pressured to give up his standards and to conform to the luring seductions of the world.

Fortunately for us, we are not thrown into the lion's den with no defense. God has given us numerous tools and much advice that we can apply in swabbing the decks of our mind. If we truly desire to be wholesome in thought, resulting in lasting behavior as a holy vessel for Christ, then we must use the cleansing agent of the Word of God to begin this process.

> *For our struggle is not against flesh and blood, but against the rulers, against the authorities, against the power of this dark world and against the spiritual forces of evil in the heavenly realms* (Ephesians 6:12).

It seems logical that if our struggle with unwholesome thinking is derived from the powers of the dark world, and Satan himself, then we need to learn from God's point of view how to go about purifying our minds for His usefulness.

CHANGE FROM THE INSIDE OUT

Jim Petersen in his book, *Lifestyle Discipleship*, says that change must occur at the core of our being—in the things we believe, in our world view. If things change there, values will follow in time, and behavior will not be far behind. Transformation comes from within, and works its way on out.[1] Focusing on changing our behavior before we change our thought processes and patterns will never really work long term. What we *think* directs what we *desire* and that affects what we actually *do* (Proverbs 23:7). We eventually do the things we constantly think about. Therefore, it's vital that we develop biblical convictions which will direct the way we think and act, rather than relying upon our feelings, which can be deceptive.

Let's examine three "swabbings" from 1 Peter 1:13 which we need to implement in our lives if we are to be men of wholesome thinking.

> *Therefore, prepare your minds for action; be self-controlled; set your hope fully on the grace to be given when Jesus Christ is revealed.*

Swabbing #1
PREPARE FOR ACTION

The King James Version says, "Gird up the loins of your mind." What does this imply? The allusion of girding the loins is the manner in which the Orientals were accustomed to dressing. They wore loose flowing robes so that when they wanted to run, fight, or work they are obliged to bind their garments close around them.[2]

To gird up your loins indicates getting ready for service, activity, or labor at any time or place. To loosen the loins denotes giving way to idleness and laziness. What condition have the loins of your mind been in—watchfulness or laziness? You see, if we're not allowing the Lord to prepare our minds for Christ-like action, then someone or something else will come along and prepare it for another type of action, guaranteed not to bring us closer to God. (See Ephesians 2:2.)

Don Otis in his book, *Trickle-Down Morality*, emphasizes the truth that wrong thinking leads to wrong action.

> As Christians we must know what God's Word says and be willing to obey, so that we do not make choices we know are wrong, and then have to develop a rationale for those choices. Doing so is a process that leads to self-deception. In Eve's case, self-deception began when she confused what looked good with what was right. When we focus exclusively on what looks good, we assume it must be from God and are blinded to what He wants for us. Whatever produces a "bad" result is wrong. But according to this logic, our quest for a more comfortable lifestyle could lead to a questionable business deal, since we assume the "good" end must be God's blessing. In this distortion of truth, we see choices as wrong only if their desired ends are unacceptable to us. Self deception in our thinking usually begins with small things or simple instructions, but it leads to serious results—even death.[3]

We must gain and maintain control of our thought life. How do we begin that process? 1 Peter 1:14 tells us: "Do not conform to the evil desires you had when you lived in ignorance." To be conformed means to agree in thought or idea. God calls us to be different from what we were before we accepted Christ. The best way to stay on course is to gird our minds with the Word of Truth so we will know in advance the correct course for action. Loose ropes lead to loose sails that are powerless to take a boat to its desired destination. Loose thoughts lead to loose lifestyles that prepare you to go in a different way than you desire.

A man who intends to sail his vessel toward the Father who loves him cannot afford to get sloppy and not pay attention to following the course that has been set. Preparing our minds for action is a daily struggle, but the more we think according to the standards of His Word, the more we can recognize and resist the tactics of the enemy. Many of us keep going when we should stop and check our spiritual compass to see if we have strayed off course.

Swabbing #2
BE SELF-CONTROLLED

The way a man thinks indicates the self-control in his character (Galatians 5:22). Our thoughts can become like millstones tied around our necks if they're not brought into submission using biblical principles through the power of the Holy Spirit. We may give the impression of godly character on the outside, but it's only a matter of time before absence of godly inner self-control will be evident in our life. Assuredly, the secret thoughts, intentions, and motives of a man's heart will eventually come to the surface and be revealed. It's as true today as it was thousands of years ago, "Your sin will find you out" (Numbers 32:23). Maybe not today, or tomorrow, or even next week, but eventually those depraved thoughts will lead to depraved actions. The ability to demonstrate self-control must come through the empowerment of the Holy Spirit if we are going to win the battle over the mind.

Dennis and Dawn Wilson in their book, *Christian Parenting in the Information Age*, has given an excellent definition of *self-control*:

> The ability to cause oneself to act or think contrary to how one feels at the time. Self-control includes the thinking within an individual to peacefully restrain or dismiss oneself when enticing, or negative freedoms are presented.[4]

Self-control is a moral virtue. That is, other virtues are dependent on it. It influences kindness, gentleness, how we love, and many other behaviors. When we allow the Word of God to train and equip our conscience, the result will be a moral response rather than an amoral one.

A man's self-control must be based on some authority higher than his own logical thinking. It must stem from a moral standard, a perfect standard, a biblical standard. When biblical standards are studied and obeyed, the results will be a conscience and a lifestyle governed by the standard of truth rather than what feels good.

A man shared with me over breakfast one morning, "I lack the self-control that Jesus speaks of in Scripture. I am amazed how grotesque and wicked my thinking can become when I let my mind idly wander. It's like putting my brain on 'auto pilot,' yet not having a care of where it's taking me or who is in control. That scares me. The images, scenarios, and motives that come to the forefront of my mind are so grievous at times that it must bring Christ to tears. I am certain that Christ is more concerned about renewing my mind than I truly am. What a wretched man that I am."

A disciplined man of sound mind follows sound reason. He is not under the strongholds of sexual passions, lusts, negative schemes, and motives (Ecclesiastes 7:29). He seeks to control his mind by the incorruptible seed of God's Word (1 Peter 1:23). That doesn't mean he's going to be perfect in his thoughts every day (or should I say every hour), but it does challenge him to draw on the indwelling power of the Holy Spirit to give him the strength and guidance to dismiss and replace those thoughts by making them obedient to Christ (2 Corinthians 10:5). (We'll address this concept of "dismiss and replace" in the next chapter.)

How serious are you about being God's man? Serious enough to develop the virtue of self-control in your life to the point of restoring a consistent, godly consciousness and perspective? I heard a man say, "A man without self-control in his life is like a man who lives in a paper house and decides to take up torch juggling. Eventually he will get burned, and so will everything around him."

You and I know how brutally we can be attacked through our thoughts. I have found that we're just as vulnerable to Satan's poisonous darts while asleep as we are when awake. Sitting in front of the idiot box till 11:00 at night to watch some hideous show will have profound effects on your sleeping patterns and dream state.

When discussing this issue of developing self-control with a friend, he commented on the mental battle that goes on when he is asleep. "My dreams at times are so evil, sexual, perverted, and violent, that when I wake up in a cold sweat I immediately know who's trying to win the battle for my mind!"

When fleshly thoughts come, ask yourself the following questions:
• Why am I thinking these thoughts?
• Where are these thoughts coming from (identify the source)?
• What is the danger of entertaining the thoughts of the flesh, which are trying to pepper my conscience?
• How will this kind of thinking affect the character of Christ, which God is earnestly working to develop in my life?
• Who do I wish to be mastered by?
• What biblical arsenal and strategy have I developed to take captive these thoughts?
• How might I be rationalizing my thinking and actions?

Swabbing #3
THE GRACE OF GOD

We must set our hope fully on His grace. The word I want to emphasize here is "fully." Not partially, not most of the time, but *fully* setting our hope on the grace of God. A man who is of purpose and order knows that to maintain a life of self-control he must set his hope "fully on the grace to be given when Jesus Christ is revealed" (1 Peter 1:13).

I know of many men who have had tons of aspirations, dreams, goals, and ambitions only to have them capsize due to their hope being placed in the temporal things of this earth (1 John 2:15-17). They grow faint and weary in their thinking and living for Christ and eventually abandon the hope of the grace of God.

Charles Swindoll in his book, *The Grace Awakening,* explains the reason why we should be so grateful for the grace of God.

> Please understand, to be justified does not mean "just as if I'd never sinned." I hear that often and it always troubles me. In fact, it weakens the full impact of justification. Justification really means this: Even though I still sin periodically and have found myself unable to stop sinning on a permanent basis, God

declared me righteous when I believed. And because I will continue to sin from time to time, I find all the more reason to be grateful for grace. As a sinner, I deserve vengeance. As a sinner, I'm afraid of justice. And so, as a sinner, my only hope for survival is grace. [5]

When we experience and remember the grace of our heavenly Father through His Son's death, burial, and resurrection, it should put astounding hope and joy in our souls to strive for a consistent and wholesome lifestyle until He returns.

What are you placing your hope in today? Is it all consuming? But will it last? Will it fill the void and vacuum that may reside in that heart of yours? People in trouble often say, "I don't want to get my hopes up." Yes! Get them up! The Scriptures promise in Romans 5:5 that "Hope does not disappoint us, because God has poured out His love into our hearts by the Holy Spirit, whom He has given us." We have good reason to hope that God is wise enough to make something beautiful out of our messed-up lives. Take a moment and recommit your thoughts and actions to the lordship of Jesus Christ. It's only through, by, and in His grace that we will be filled!

May I challenge you for a moment to seriously take responsibility for your thoughts by implementing the following for the next 30 days?

1. *Make a covenant* (Job 31:1; Ecclesiastes 5:4-7). As you walk out of the house each morning, commit to the Lord that you will seek to look, hear, walk, and touch only those things which are wholesome and honorable to Him.

2. *Feed on the Word of God* (Psalm 34:8; 1 Peter 2:3). For a half hour before you go to bed, digest the Word rather than going to bed with a mind cluttered with the seduction and deception that the world can throw at you from the T.V./media.

3. *Pray scripture back to the Lord* (Proverbs 23:7; Lamentations 3:21-22). As you commute to work, as you stand at the grocery checkout line, as you stand in the shower, when a certain temptation arises— these are just a few of the many times you can meditate on and pray back to God what you have placed in the storehouse of your mind.

4. *Listen to Christian music* as a part of your day (Ephesians 5:19-20; Colossians 3:15-17). Ask the Lord to cleanse your mind and heart through praise and worship. Singing praises to Him restores our thinking and gives us the confidence to persevere as holy men of faith.

5. *Read uplifting and wholesome literature.* One of the best tools to help us begin to develop biblical thinking is to read the fruitful words of Christian writers. As you read how God used others, you will be encouraged and challenged to believe that God may have something special for you to do.

God is jealous for our minds (Deuteronomy 4:24). He labors night and day for the sacredness of a clean mind for you and me. He is not willing to share our hearts and minds with anyone or anything. He will go to any extent, any extreme, to bring all things under subjection of His lordship. The question is, do you have the same passion for pureness of thought as the Lord has for you?

> *Rather clothe yourselves with the Lord Jesus Christ, and do not think about how to gratify the desires of the sinful nature* (Romans 13:14).

CHARTING YOUR COURSE

SELF-EVALUATION

1. What is the danger of entertaining the thoughts of the flesh, which try to pepper your conscience?

2. As you strive to develop the mind of Christ this week, take some time to meditate on the following. . .
   Set your mind—Romans 8:5-8; Philippians 4:8; Colossians 3:2
   (Stage of beginning/focus)
   Renew your mind—Romans 12:1-2
   (Stage of transformation/change)
   Gird up your mind—1 Peter 1:13
   (Stage of strategy)

3. What thoughts of the past does the enemy try to derail you with, in order to discourage or defeat you as a growing believer in Christ?

4. What biblical arsenal and strategy have you developed to take captive the thoughts of the flesh? (See Romans 12:1-2; 2 Corinthians 10:5-6; Colossians 3:15-17.)

GROUP DISCUSSION
1. In what ways can you prepare your mind for action on a daily basis?

2. Group Exercise: Anonymously, on a 3x5 index card, have each man write down where they are most susceptible in getting picked off by the enemy. Collect them, shuffle them up, and then write out the responses on a blackboard for all the men to see. Then discuss:

- What do these responses tell us about the tactics of the enemy?
- What do these responses tell us about our struggles?
- What do these responses tell us about our thought life?
- What does this tell us about the body of Christ?

Music Resources: "Cleanse Me", by Charles Wesley
"*Refine Me,*" on the Jennifer Knapp-*Kansas* CD

Sources
[1] Jim Petersen, *Lifestyle Discipleship,* Christian Business Men's Committee; Chattanooga, Tennessee 1993, pp.82-84.

[2] Albert Barnes, *Barnes Notes on the New Testament* (Baker Book House, Grand Rapids, Michigan, reprinted from the 1884-85 edition published by Blackie and Son), p.126.

[3] Don S. Otis, *Trickle-Down Morality* (Chosen Books, A division of Baker Book House Grand Rapids, Michigan 1998), p.45.

[4] Dennis and Dawn Wilson, *Christian Parenting in the Information Age* (Tri Cord Pub. Sierra Vista, Arizona, 1996), p.62.

[5] Charles R. Swindoll, *The Grace Awakening* (Word Pub. Dallas, Texas, 1990), p.42.

Chapter 12
PIRATES ON THE HORIZON

"Some have in fact already turned away to follow Satan."
—1 Timothy 5:15

The sky is clear, and the wind is soft as a mink coat. Your voyage today couldn't be better. Conditions are perfect. Nothing, it would seem, could get in the way of your voyage to the mainland. Then suddenly, out of nowhere, comes a ship. From a distance it looks like any other ship—sails well trimmed, activity aboard, and a flag on the main mast. Wait a second, that's not just any flag, that's the flag of a pirate ship! Skull and cross bones on its cloth—a picture of the enemy, a picture of death. What was to be a flawless adventure this afternoon is now postponed as fear grips your heart because the enemy is sailing straight for you. As the ship gets close, you can see the cold glint of their swords and hear the roughness in their voices. They've been around for a long time. They know the territory, and they know what they want. They want to overcome you and make you their slave.

Satan has a way of gripping us with fear and trepidation, doesn't he? He's ruthless and will go to any extreme to interrupt and confuse your day or week. Scripture paints a very vivid picture of Satan and his overall purpose in wanting to shipwreck your life.

Be on your guard and stay awake. Your enemy, the devil, is like a roaring lion, sneaking around to find someone to attack. But you must resist the devil and stay strong in your faith (1 Peter 5:8-9 CEV).

I remember traveling through West Virginia with a friend. As we drove along, we passed a huge sign advertising the location of a Triple X adult video/bookstore. We laughed when we went by (and we did drive quickly past) and saw that the name of the porno store was *The Lions Den*. I said to Jim, "How fitting. They don't realize how scriptural they really are."

But why a lion? Why does Peter describe the devil as a roaring lion? Maybe this will help. The head of the Los Angeles Zoo was asked, "Why do lions roar?" Here are the reasons he gave:

1. They are hungry.

2. They want to paralyze you with fear and intimidation.

3. They want to expand their territory.

Guess what? The devil prowls around for the very same reasons. Satan is hungry, and because he's your enemy and the enemy of Christ, he's hungry for you. He will take you out without notice because that's his battle plan. But it's really not about you and me, is it? We're just little pawns in a bigger game of war. It's about trying to destroy the Name above all names, the King of kings and Lord of lords—Jesus Christ. If Satan can keep our faith, marriage, integrity, or purity from maintaining a correct course of righteousness, then he can gain more territory that was once in the kingdom of God.

Satan's hunger to trip us up and defile the name of Christ is never quenched, and he will be ruthless until he's thrown into the lake of fire for all eternity (Revelation 20:10). Every temptation that Satan throws at us seeks in some way to tarnish or rot our character, whether that be through the love of money, pride, sexual immorality, or whatever. But make no mistake about it, he's after you! As you read this, Satan at this very point in time is eating at some of you.

Satan wants us to be ineffective and fearful of him. Have you ever said, "God, I just can't take one more step," because you can feel and smell the enemy's breath on the back of your neck? Satan loves to paralyze us so our marriage, ministry, parenting, and walk with Christ will become ineffective. He wants to keep us from staying on course and reaching our destination. The good news is that over 300 times in Scripture, God tells us to not fear for He is with us. God Himself is fighting and praying for us to stay on course and to not deviate from the plans He has for us. He provides many things—His Word, another brother in Christ, or a word of encouragement from someone—to help us fight against Satan's paralyzing grip.

I love the picture in a local pizza shop near my house that shows seven iron workers high above the city taking an afternoon nap. As you look at it, you have to laugh because all seven of them in some way have their legs hooked around another man for support. It's like they're saying, "If one begins to fall, together we'll keep him from falling. We're in this together. Each one of us is too valuable to lose so we're going to hold on to each other." Wow! Do you have others like that, who don't give up on you and will help keep you from falling? *Together* we can ride the crest of the waves to safe passage.

Satan wants to expand his territory. He'll give us the false illusion that what he offers is greater than what the One who looks out for us night and day has for us. Satan is desperately trying to move into our homes, ministries, and personal lives with the hope that he can gain permanent territory. If we know Christ as Savior, we know that the enemy can't take our soul. He will, however, go to any extreme to wreak havoc on our lives if we leave even the slightest gap open for him to worm his way in. When the enemy draws up beside your boat, it's time to call out the fleet and fight together.

How can we protect ourselves against the enemy when he sails into our territory and is looking to stir up some trouble?

KEEPING THINGS SHIPSHAPE

Several years ago my wife and I went on a seven-day cruise. It was spectacular. From the moment we entered the ship, we were awestruck by how clean, crisp, and elegant everything was. As we enjoyed a week of tanning in the sun with not a care in the world, hundreds of employees around us and below us were constantly making sure that the cruise ship was shipshape externally and internally.

It was a tight ship. Beds were made on time, floors were always swept, and the food was magnificent. We couldn't help but walk away and be impressed with the vessel that wined and dined us all week, and then safely brought us back to the mainland.

What's *your* vessel looking like? Do you run a tight ship? Is your mind crisp and clean for the Captain of your soul?

If we are going to have a vessel that is shipshape, then we need to develop some measurable parameters which will cleanse our mind and not clutter it. Do you have some boundaries, which are *non-negotiable,* that you have set down to guard your thoughts? Here are a few to consider:

• Time in the Word (Psalm 119:105).
• Places you have decided are off limits for you to go (1 Peter 1:13).
• Refusing to give in to the listening or telling of a dirty joke (Proverbs 22:15).
• People you might have to disengage from because of harmful influence (1 Corinthians 15:33).

It is so much easier to set parameters than to run the risk of having to pick up the pieces after you have given in to carnal thinking and living. Charles Spurgeon said it best,

> Our thoughts, if left to themselves, are likened to a cage of unclean birds or a den of wild beasts. Christ desires to pour rivers of water out of His own heart to cleanse the foul stable of our corrupt thoughts.[1]

DISMISS AND REPLACE

Satan subtly disguises his crafty voice and masquerades as an angel of light (2 Corinthians 11:14), whispering in our ear the lie, "It's just one look, just one thought, just one last time…"

I've heard that whisper, and so have you. Satan loves to creep into our thoughts when we are spiritually burned out, emotionally depressed, and physically overworked, casting temptation into our weakened condition.

As a former youth pastor, I remember being told after I had just come off a mountaintop experience on a missions trip with our teens, "A soldier is most vulnerable after victory." I thought, *How could the enemy attack me now? I'm at the top of my spiritual walk. I've seen God do mighty things in our teens lives and in my life over the course of the last week. It's just not possible that the enemy could get a foothold. The walls of righteousness are just too high right now.* How little I understood of Satan's ways at that time!

What I didn't know is that Satan is a master at digging under my "wall of righteousness" and slithering into my thinking. He strategically used my great experience with God to give me an overwhelming self-confidence, thinking I could not fall for his tactics. How wrong I was! I had stepped into the trap he had masterfully camouflaged, making evil look innocent and harmless. Instead of dismissing the thoughts he threw at me, I gave way to them and missed out on a wonderful opportunity to be blessed and grow. Rather than replace and demolish these strongholds by the divine power of Jesus Christ, I fell right into the enemy's trap.

For though we live in the world, we do not wage war as the world does. The weapons we fight with are not the weapons of the world; on the contrary, they have divine power to demolish strongholds. We must take captive every thought to make it obedient to Christ (2 Corinthians 10:3-5). How do we do it? Paul, in Philippians 4:8, helps us navigate this course by giving us solid biblical coordinates to dismiss every unwholesome thought and replace it with a godly one.

DISMISS	REPLACE WITH
Falsehood	Whatever is TRUE
Disrespect	Whatever is NOBLE
Dishonest gain	Whatever is RIGHT
Pervertedness	Whatever is PURE
Malice/criticism	Whatever is LOVELY
Judgmental attitudes	Whatever is EXCELLENT/PRAISEWORTHY

Paul gives us the result of "dismiss and replace" when he says, "Think about such things. Whatever you have learned and received or heard from me, or seen in me, put it into practice. And the God of peace will be with you" (Philippians 4:8-9).

The greatest joy in replacing unwholesome thoughts with newness of thought and life is the peace of God. There is an overwhelming sense of having done (practiced) what will bring Him glory and honor instead of caving in to carnal thinking.

To dismiss and replace is not easy; it never has been. But when our passion is to stand in the gap and be men of valor rather than men who jump ship, we begin to develop a healthy, righteous, and God-honoring conscience.

Biblical study that results in increased self-control must be our first choice instead of our last grab for stability. It's like riding a bike for the first time without training wheels—there are going to be some bumps, scrapes, and bruises along the way, but eventually we develop a stronger assurance of our capabilities. Little by little we begin to see some progress in making biblically based decisions we know to be correct and true rather than taking careless risks which may scar our life and character.

Don't disqualify yourself before you even get out of harbor. Be the man who, on any given day, can pull up anchor while in harbor and cruise out into deeper waters. Take the time to discipline your mind to be a vessel worthy of the calling that the Captain of your soul has placed on you.

Take a moment and evaluate how you might take captive every thought to make it obedient to Christ. We must guard our thoughts regarding: our past, our present condition, the future, ourself, others, our faith in Christ.

CHARTING YOUR COURSE

SELF-EVALUATION

1. In what way has this chapter helped you to see the importance "dismiss and replace" (Philippians 4:8) must have in your life if you are to maintain a pattern of wholesome thinking?

2. Satan, like a fierce lion, seeks to devour his prey. In what ways are you prepared when he roams into your territory?

Video Resource: *Personal Holiness in Times of Temptation*, by Dr. Bruce H. Wilkinson. This is an excellent video series, which has helped in transforming many men in our church to be men who seek after holiness rather than flirting with temptation or yielding to a fleeting moment of sin. It is very helpful in taking biblical steps toward sexual purity. This video series can be purchased through:Walk Thru The Bible Ministries, Inc., 4201 North Peachtree Road, Atlanta, GA 30341 (800) 763-5433.

Source
[1] Tom Carter, *Spurgeon At His Best* (Grand Rapids, Michigan: Baker Book House, 1988), p.13.

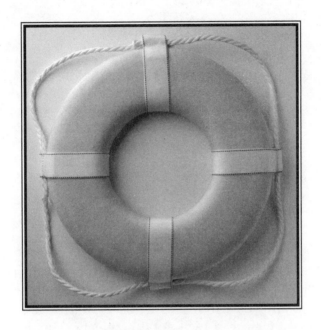

COORDINATE #5

Navigating
Toward
Sexual Purity

Chapter 13

RUNNING AGROUND

"Some have rejected these and so have shipwrecked their faith" (1 Timothy 1:19).

Who could ever forget the tragic event in March, 1989, when the Exxon Valdes ran aground in Prince William Sound in the Gulf of Alaska, spilling 11 million gallons of crude oil? Hundreds of thousands of fish and seabirds died from the accident, which could have been avoided if the captain had used good judgment. Hundreds of fisherman and residents suffered from the worst oil spill in U.S. history— many had to move and find employment elsewhere.

Sin has a way of doing the same devastating thing in our lives. The reefs that can cause us to run aground are dangerous indeed, not just for us, but for the many others whose lives are connected to ours. Our Christian testimony can be destroyed in an instant when we stray from the course set out for us.

Over and over again, I've observed and read about faithful men who have run aground and shipwrecked their lives and character by sexual sins. It seems as if this is the cannonball that the enemy loves to catapult our way to destroy us. Many men are neglecting to stay alert to the tactics of the enemy and are getting sidetracked by pornography and adulterous affairs. This even includes men in the pastorate who have been called by God to lead other individuals to safe waters.

Frederick Buechner said it best:

Lust is the ape that gibbers in our loins. Tame him as we will by day, he rages all the wilder in our dreams by night. Just when we think we're safe from him, he raises up his ugly head and smirks. There is no river in the world which flows cold and strong enough to strike him down. Almighty God, why doest thou deck men out with such a loathsome toy?[1]

Strong words, aren't they? It makes us feel uneasy when we read it, but our spirit says, how true it is. The following is a question that I'm finding men asking me over and over: "Is there freedom that I can have over these unbridled, lustful passions that seem to be raging out of control and heading me toward disaster?" The answer is yes, but it's not easy. Freedom does not mean the absence of a potential collision, but the avoidance of it.

I'm not going to load you down or bore you with the latest statistics on sexual indulgence in our culture today. Nor am I going to waste time with one story after another of how men have become entrapped by and addicted to this poison of uncontrollable lust. We are well aware of the reality of this already happening in our nation.

I do, however, want to ask why men are dropping out of the fleet and jeopardizing their families, reputations, faith, and conscience (1 Timothy 1:18-19) by chasing after the ruthless enemy of sexual indulgence. In order to navigate our lives toward biblical manhood, we need to have a well-defined plan that will not bring us down, slow us up, or keep us from maintaining a correct course to sexual purity.

We are reminded by Paul in Galatians 5:7-10 to make sure that no one or nothing distracts our attention and knocks us off course:

You were doing so well until someone made you turn from the truth. And that person was certainly not sent by the One who chose you. A little yeast can change a whole batch of dough, but you belong to the Lord (CEV)

We must stop rationalizing our actions, for by doing so we play right into the devil's hands. This results in paralysis of the soul and cripples any trust factor we may have established in our personal relationships. Making excuses for our sin by wrapping it up and putting a pretty bow on it does not make it any less offensive in God's eyes, nor should it be in ours. We try to justify our behavior, but our heavenly Father is just in His behavior.

SENDING UP A FLARE

For most of us it's an everyday (maybe every hour or every minute) battle to keep lustful passions under control. The long process it takes for a man to be delivered from the internal war with sexual passions is neither easy nor pleasant, and most certainly will stretch our relationships for a time. Why is it that when all of our resources are diminished, all of our options are spent, and we are lost with little or no idea of how to get home, we finally push our male ego aside and resort to prayer? Like a bright flare being sent up at night so those around may see, so is the distress signal of a broken man crying to God for help. When the hull of our vessel is quickly going under, and we are seriously thinking about abandoning ship, we need more than the coast guard to come and save our hides.

No quick fix, and no person outside of Jesus Christ is going to deliver us from this entrapment. We cannot put our sins behind us until we are ready to face them. If we're playing games and not going to come clean and recognize our need for help, then the solutions I'm going to offer are unavailing. Charles Spurgeon said, "There can be no such thing as perfect peace till there is perfect purity." We must be alert and on guard, but how?

Let me give you several flares that will illuminate your darkened path as you seek to sail back into safe waters.

1. *Recognize your need for help.* The first step to recover in any area of life is to admit you are sick and in need of a remedy. Until you do this, you will be easy prey for the enemy.

2. *Know the prime times when you are vulnerable.* Don't become ignorant of how the enemy subtly moves in to distract you at certain times and gets you to rush in where angels dare not go.

3. *Look beyond the temptation to the consequences.* We are not talking about a slap on the wrist for having our hand in the cookie jar. We are talking about lives being destroyed, character being tossed to the wind,

and a wife and kids who will be scarred because of our foolishness in not keeping in step with the Holy Spirit's convicting and guiding power (Galatians 5:25). In Steve Green's contemporary Christian song, "Guard Your Heart," he warns us of the dangers of being swayed by our emotions rather than deciding in advance to do the right thing. (See Prov. 4:23.) The key to sexual freedom is to have a well thought out strategy of knowing what to do or not to do, way in advance.

4. *Your view of Christ and of sin must change.* When you and I sin, it proves that we're not content with what Christ offered to us on Calvary through His shed blood. Do you love your sin more than the Savior? If you do, then you must change. Are you grieved by your sin? And if you are, does it stir you to true repentance resulting in biblical purity? It's amazing what sin costs us in our relationship with Christ. It costs us blessings, rewards, opportunities to be stretched, fellowship, a clean heart to worship and praise His name, and so much more. Men, it's just not worth it! Besides, it's difficult to sing "A Mighty Fortress Is Our God" when we've been looking at pornography all week.

5. *A change of mind is in order.* A change of mind results in a change of heart. Remember the theme that runs throughout the book of Judges in the Old Testament? "And the nation of Israel did what was right in their own eyes..." They lacked the wisdom and discernment to make godly choices which Proverbs 3 speaks so deeply about.

6. *Your desire to be pure and honor your relationships must become greater than a fleeting moment of indulgence.* Your hunger to know Him, thirst after Him, and follow Him must be all consuming. To be pure in heart is the trademark of a holy vessel.

Blessed are the pure in heart for they will see God (Matthew 5:8).

7. *Develop a balanced diet of the Word of God, the Spirit's guidance, and counsel from godly men.* They will grab an oar and help you row through this time of brokenness, to a time of breaking through the dark clouds to newness of life.

How can a young man keep his way pure? By living according to Your Word. I seek You with all my heart; do not let me stray from

Your commands. I have hidden Your Word in my heart that I might not sin against You (Psalm 119:9-11).

Flee from sexual immorality. All other sins a man commits are outside His body, but he who sins sexually sins against his own body. Do you not know that your body is a temple of the Holy Spirit, who is in you, whom you have received from God? You are not your own; you were bought at a price. Therefore honor God with your body (1 Corinthians 6:18-20).

If you have sinned, you should tell each other what you have done. Then you can pray for one another and be healed. The prayer of an innocent person is powerful, and it can help a lot (James 5:16 CEV).

8. *Determine a plan before the temptation rears its ugly head.* Learn to stop the drifting process at the earliest possible stage. Gain self-control before the sexual drive gains strength and takes control over you (1 Peter 1:13). You must deal with sin, or sin will deal with you! (Genesis 4:7)

9. *Begin to clean house.* Are there things in your home or at work that can be a temptation? They need to go. Don't rationalize them, just get rid of them! We wouldn't let a cobra into our home, because it's deadly. Likewise, let's get rid of or flee from anything that can be a potential poison in our life. Let's determine what excess cargo needs to be tossed (see 2 Chronicles 29; 1 Thessalonians 4:3-8). Viewing sexually explicit material or becoming involved in an affair has "collision course" written all over it (Proverbs 7:1-27).

10. *Rekindle the fear of God once again.* Begin to practice the presence of God in your life. Bill Gothard says, "Fearing God is the conscious awareness that He is watching everything and evaluating everything we think, say, and do." That will either make you incredibly confident in saying, "Yes, Lord, I am a clean vessel. Thank you for making me whole and guiding my course daily as I become Christ-like," or it will make you feel very uncomfortable because the life you've been living is not under the direct orders of the One you claim to know and love. He knows what is going on deep down inside the hull of our hearts, and He knows whether we are sincere about dealing with and getting rid of

these sexual binges that can bring spiritual and physical death to our soul. Just as Joshua said to his people in Joshua 24:14-15, "Choose this day whom you will serve," God is asking you and me to do the same. Guard your heart, brother—I'll watch your back. Would you be a friend and watch mine as well?

When victory and freedom over this bitter sin is achieved, we can, with a clear conscience, lay our head on our pillow at night with the satisfaction that we made the right choice in an amoral culture. In the end, it will bring freedom to the soul and restoration with our Lord. "So if the Son has set you free, you will be free indeed" (John 10:10).

 CHARTING YOUR COURSE

SELF-EVALUATION
1. Are there any improper videos, magazines, etc., in your home?

2. When and where are you most susceptible to sexual immorality? Do you have a well thought out strategy to overcome the temptations?

GROUP DISCUSSION
1. Why has the sexual sin of pornography become the "worst kept secret" among many Christian men in our culture today?

Reading Resource: Mark Laaser Ph.D., *Faithful & True* (Zondervan Publishing).

Video Resource: *Leave Your Jacket* by John Maxwell, delivered at Promise Keepers in Indianapolis, IN.

Music Resource: "*Clumsy*" by Chris Rice off *Deep Enough to Dream CD*.

Source
[1] "The War Within," *Leadership Magazine*, Fall Quarter, 1992, p.97.

Chapter 14

LOGBOOKS OF SHIPWRECKED VESSELS

"A collision at sea can ruin your entire day"—Thucydides

The following are actual testimonies of men around this country who are struggling to keep afloat in spite of the overwhelming pressures to gratify the lustful passions that lie beneath the surface of the skin:

"I try to suppress it (which lasts for a week, maybe two) then it comes exploding to the surface with such force and enticement that I am like a wild animal on a quest to fill my stomach (this void) with anything that will satisfy the passion for a period of time."

"I confess this grotesque sin to God. I really mean it! Yet in a moment of numbness, I find myself leafing through a dirty book, grazing through a porno store, or throwing quarters in a 'chick flick' as fast as I can feed them, to get one more moment of unfulfilled teasing. For when my quarters are gone, I am both satisfied and empty, always desiring more."

"It's a food that many feast on, gorge themselves on, and many have choked to their death on."

"You are well aware it destroys your character, yet you risk it, go for broke and continue on your binge of flesh. It will destroy your relationship with your heavenly Father—yet you continue in what many refer to as 'mindless feeding.'"

"It will bring to death the life and love of your marriage—yet you continue to hide it, giving the impression of holiness but internally knowing better."

"There are days when I would much rather accept the fires of hell, than for my wife and kids to ever find out about my losing battle with pornography."

"I hate who I am. I hate my sin. I hate the passion to lust, to look, to mentally have intercourse with a piece of paper that has a flawless picture of a nude woman on it. I am in a dungeon, and I am my own worst enemy. My God, that's someone's daughter! That's someone's mother! God, what is wrong with me? I am out of control! I am not what I ought to be, I need help."

"Kings have renounced their thrones, saints their God, and spouses their lifetime partners because of this ruthless demon of lust."

"The longer I hide it, try to control it by myself, the more I am awakened to the fact that it will eventually come out, and when it does, it won't be pretty—but I know it will result in a freedom I have yet to experience."

"I am a businessman. My job takes me out of town quite frequently. For 25 years I have struggled with pornography. I know what not to do. Yet I find myself in places and doing things that I know to be not only wrong, but evil. My conscience screams at me to get out of there, to flee, to run, yet I linger and secretly plan and look for windows of opportunity; justifying my actions every step of the way. It's like making a date with a snake. How quickly my flesh says indulge, while my spirit cries WITHDRAW!"

"With the struggle of lust, it is not an issue of how much or how little, but an issue of hiding that lust from valuable relationships with those who love me more than I love myself."

"I could handle lust better if I knew it would strike me in October or May. It's the not knowing, the ceaseless vulnerability, that drives me crazy."

DON'T DRINK THAT WATER

I read an illustration not too long ago about a vessel that had become shipwrecked. Men were left drifting aimlessly on the ocean in a lifeboat. As the days passed under the scorching sun, their rations of food and fresh water ran out. The men grew deliriously thirsty. One night while the others were asleep, a man ignored all previous warnings and gulped down some salt water. He quickly died. Ocean water contains seven times more salt than the human body can safely digest. By drinking it, a person dehydrates because the kidneys demand fresh water to flush and purify the overload of salt. The more salt water someone drinks, the thirstier they become until the person actually dies of thirst. When we lust after another woman, we become like this shipwrecked man—we thirst desperately for something that looks like what we want. We don't realize, however, that it is precisely the opposite of what we really need. In fact, it will kill us. If tombstones could talk, many would give serious warnings against this deadly sin.

Solomon's advice to men of all nations for all times is perfectly clear regarding adultery:

> *Drink water from your own cistern, running water from your own well. Should your springs overflow in the streets, your streams of water in the public squares? Let them be yours alone, never to be shared with strangers. May your fountain be blessed, and may you rejoice in the wife of your youth. A loving doe, a graceful deer— may her breast satisfy you always, may you ever be captivated by her love. Why be captivated, my son, by an adulteress? Why embrace the bosom of another man's wife? For a man's ways are in full view of the Lord, and He examines all his paths* (Proverbs 5:15-21).

For some of us, we know that if we cross over into the enemy waters of pornography or adultery, it can be fatal. The loss of a ministry, marriage, or character is nothing to be flirting with. You and I have observed others who have sailed right into the eye of the hurricane, putting their vessel into a tail spin of despair and helplessness. My advice to you is to stay clean. Keep drinking from the cup of the one to whom you made wedding vows. Let's not forget the taste of what true love is all about. Let's keep our ear attentive to the advice of the One who stands in the crow's nest.

Some reading this have crossed the line and dabbled with pornography or thoughts of adultery. They were so convicted by what they experienced and shocked by the darkness of sexual entrapment that they wised up quickly and left well enough alone. Stay away and guard your heart (Proverbs 4:23).

There are also those of you who are currently being marooned by the enemy. You are calling out for help, for a trusted friend who can come to your aid and offer support and guidance without judgmental or self-righteous overtones. By the grace of God may you begin to take wholesome steps back to righteous living. "Though you can't go back and make a brand new start, anyone can start from now and make a brand new end" (John Maxwell).

Finally there are those of us, who, after all the warnings, are lured time and time again to succumb to the temptations of sexual sins. Though harpooned and bleeding, we continue to hide our shame and act out the drama of life as if all is well. Knowing it will bring about the death of our family, marriage, personal integrity, and walk with Christ, we continue to walk the plank and look over the edge. If I'm speaking to you, and you don't get help soon, there will come a day when you will walk out on the plank and plunge to your death in a sea of pain, grief, and isolation. You need the healing power of Christ and others to offer a lasting love that you have yet to find. Don't wait until your vessel sinks to the bottom before you sound the alarm for help.

BEHIND THE DOOR
The shelf behind the door,
  the shelf behind the door,
Tear it down and throw it out,
  don't use it anymore.
For Jesus wants His temple clean,
  from ceiling to the floor,
He even wants that little shelf,
  that's hid behind the door.
By Vance Havner

The rule of thumb is that nobody will ever ask to see your log book until you get into trouble. Let's make sure our vessel remains clean, as we navigate our lives toward biblical purity.

SECOND CHANCES

Ever wanted, needed, or gotten a second chance? You're forever grateful when you do. Life is filled with second chances. It's a process of getting up, falling down and getting up again, yet all the while moving closer to the Lord. God is the distributor of those second chances. He is the God, in fact, whose mercy endureth forever (1 Chronicles 16:34). It's never cut off. It's like the Energizer Bunny. His mercy keeps going and going and going. I'm thankful for second chances when I know I have sinned, made an unwise decision, or wounded a close friend due to my lack of discernment. If there is one word in Scripture that demonstrates the awesomeness of God's mercy for His children, it would have to be the word. . . "again." The word denotes "once more," or an action to be repeated.

> *And when they cried out to You again, You heard from heaven, and in Your compassion You delivered them time after time* (Nehemiah 9:28).

> *Though You have made me see trouble, many and bitter, You will restore my life again; from the depths of the earth You will again bring me up. You will increase my honor and comfort me once again* (Psalm 71:20-21).

> *Restore us again, O God our Savior, and put away Your displeasure toward us. Will You not revive us again, that Your people may rejoice in You* (Psalm 85:4,6).

> *And again, I will put my trust in Him. And again He says, Here am I, and the children God has given me* (Hebrews 2:13).

Does God hold onto such children whose confidence has been shattered due to worldly living, lustful passions, or unwise decisions? You bet He does!

God's second chances of mercy and grace are our one route to freedom from the confusion, guilt, shame, and self-doubt that hammers at our sanity.

With His mercy and grace comes the outpouring of His love and forgiveness. It's our escape from the ruthless accusations the enemy screams in our direction, telling us we are no good, or unworthy to call ourselves a follower of Christ. Our response is to pour out our sin and repent of our wrong, and to then move on learning a hard lesson from our foolish behavior. That doesn't mean we take advantage of His grace and mercy. It does mean, however, that it's available when we have run aground and we need His restoring Spirit to keep us pure in an age of compromise.

• For all the Jonahs who have ever neglected God's calling to come out of their comfort zone. . . a second chance is waiting.

• For all the John Marks who have lost self-confidence because of letting down or deserting a friend. . . He's got great plans in store for you.

• For all the Davids who have blown it due to sexual, ethical, or moral sin, and feel worthless and guilt-ridden. . . God is waiting around the corner to restore you with open arms.

• For all the Jacobs who have tried to manipulate their way through life. . . It may take a night of wrestling with God before you surrender and make things right with those you've wronged.

The unmasking of ourselves is a necessary part of God's process of healing. We must endure its pain and look forward to the relief that will surely follow. God knows that pain is the greatest motivator to change. It's a sad fact, but a true one. People change faster when they hurt than under almost any other condition. And change is what God is about in the end. He has no desire to fry us in the heat of exposure; He means to bring us to a new day, a new beginning, a second chance. In fact, He may even have a surprise up His sleeve that will make positive use of our pain and struggle—once again!

The mighty Niagara River plummets some 180 feet at the American and Horseshoe Falls. Before you get to the falls, there are violent, turbulent rapids. Farther upstream, however, where the river's current flows more gently, boats are able to navigate. Just before the Welland River empties into the Niagara, a pedestrian walkway spans the river. Posted on this bridge's pylons is a warning sign for all boaters. DO YOU HAVE AN ANCHOR? Followed by, DO YOU

KNOW HOW TO USE IT? If we neglect to use the anchor of God's Word to conquer the violent and turbulent rapids of lust, we will eventually find ourselves downstream and, in time, going over the falls.

➤ CHARTING YOUR COURSE ➤

SELF-EVALUATION
1. How do you feel when you're tempted to commit a sexual sin?

2. How can the pain of confronting and dealing with areas we have avoided, neglected, or pushed down over a period of time bring us to a point of freedom?

3. How would you finish the statement: "If given a second chance, I wish I could go back and. . ."

GROUP DISCUSSION
1. Why does God so mercifully give us second chances when we usually don't deserve it? What does that tell you about the God we serve? (See 1 Chronicles 16:34; Lamentations 3:55-56.)

2. According to Proverbs 6:20-35, what will eventually be the results for the man who steps across biblical lines into an adulterous affair?

Video Resource: *Guard Your Heart* Video Series by Dr. Gary Rosberg. The video you will want to ask for is *Ultimate Sexuality*. This is a gripping video on the tragedy that occurs when an affair takes place. This video will shake you to the core and cause you to stay away from the fire of adultery. See chapter 2 for information on how to order this video series.

Reading Resource: *False Intimacy—Understanding the Struggle of Sexual Addiction* by Dr. Harry W. Schaumburg (NavPress, Colorado Springs, Colorado 1997).

Navigating
Our Marriage and Family

Chapter 15

MUTINY ON THE HOME FRONT

Invest in your children today and reap the rewards for a lifetime.

It serves to be one of the most famous sea stories of all time. It was 1787, and Lieutenant William Bligh was appointed captain of a small ship, the HMS Bounty, by Sir Joseph Banks and the British Admiralty. The goal of the voyage was to obtain a large number of breadfruit cuttings in Tahiti to be taken to the Caribbean where they would be planted to provide food for the slaves in those colonies.

The voyage was a difficult one. Living in such close quarters, ill-feelings began to evolve. Restlessness and tensions ran high among the crew and captain. After a long stay in Tahiti to gather and stow the breadfruit plantings on board, the Bounty began its voyage to the Caribbean.

Sometime, however, on the morning of April 28, 1789, twelve crew members staged the now famous mutiny, capturing the ship and setting Captain Bligh and his supporters adrift in the ship's launch.[1] In a moment of madness, order was lost, purpose was forgotten, and selfishness was set in motion.

What's going on at the home front of your family? Is there harmony among everyone or is there a mutiny in the making? I believe when Christ looks in on some homes today, He is filled with grief and sorrow when He sees the way many family members treat one another.

During tension filled counseling sessions, I've seen too many times how couples think the best solution to their domestic problems is deceptively plan some kind of mutiny within the ranks of the home to get their way or decide to call it quits. That certainly isn't the answer.

Home is where the real action is—it's not at work or even with our buddies. It's at home. It's where we roll up our sleeves and dig in with strength and tenderness. It's where we place a tremendous amount of love and value on our children, more than any TV hero or sports star ever could. It's where our character should mirror the very life of Jesus Christ. Over the years I've learned from my kids that they don't care about the raise, the promotion, or the new Lexus (okay, mini-van) that sits out in the driveway. What they need is me! What they long for is a team who will *weather* the storms of life *together*, not create them in the process. You probably already know this, but let's review Family 101 again so we can avoid any thought of mutiny on the home front along the way. Let's use banking as a picture to work with.

As fathers we need to make an investment into the lives of our children. The more we invest, the greater the return. The more we withdraw however, the more our deposits decrease, our investments begin to crash, resulting in bankruptcy. We bankrupt our children from receiving the blessings of a healthy deposit of love, care, and concern both now and in the future. Therefore, it is extremely important that we deposit and invest into their lives what I call the Four T's to a godly heritage.

Investment/Deposit #1
DADS NEED TO BE TOUGH WITH THEIR CHILDREN

I'm not talking about being harsh, overpowering, hostile, or even dictatorial. I'm saying we need dads who are willing to set and stand by the same example of biblical standards we set for our sons and daughters. We need to provide adequate and reasonable boundaries for them to function in. Giving our children reasonable boundaries will impact them for a lifetime. Notice I said *we* must set the rules. We must set the boundaries, and *we* must determine the consequences when those boundaries have been neglected or ignored. When the roles within the home are reversed and the children begin to set the pace for the home, the result will be conflict, chaos, and mass confusion. I know of a man who makes over a million dollars a year, deals with some of the strongest and most influential men in the nation, and yet he is afraid to stand up to his own son and be tough in setting boundaries.

We need to set *internal* boundaries where certain character traits, convictions, courage, and humility are laid down. These boundaries are easier for our children to understand and conform to when they see them first enforced in our own lives.

We must also be tough in setting *external* boundaries, where personal upkeep of certain disciplines, time restraints, and limitations are emphasized. If our children are not willing to be faithful in little, they should not be given the blessing and privilege to be entrusted with much (Matthew 25:21). Certain compensation should be awarded when they have proven themselves in handling responsibilities around the house, shown respect to family members, made mature decisions, and obeyed and honored those in authority.

These boundaries are not intended to confine or hinder our children's growth; they are designed to instill integrity, respect, and honor for one another. Boundaries are set to help, not hinder; to protect, not punish. Boundaries should show that you care for the well-being of your children, instead of arbitrarily setting rigid or legalistic parameters which will only exasperate them (Ephesians 6:4). When we demonstrate and communicate to our children the value of biblical boundaries in their lives, it will bring a bountiful return in the present as well as the future.

Investment/Deposit #2:
DADS NEED TO BE TENDER

Remember falling off your bike as a child? Who did you always run to? Mom, right? And when you wanted to use the car or needed money, who did you run to? Dad, right? As fathers, our tenderness or lack of it will remain in the memory bank of our children long after we are gone. Are you creating a memory bank of hugs, kisses, and encouragement that will outlive you or just a memory of your provision for their physical needs? We teach our children to be tender in touch and tone by how we treat not only them but also our wives. We are great at being men of strength and steel, but we must also learn the value of tenderness.

Timothy Wright, in his book, *A Community of Joy*, shows the priority that touch needs to have on those within our home and within our church who are in pain and need the loving arms of another to wrap around them.

A pastor was touring a children's unit of a large Southern California hospital. Walking down the hallway, he could hear the cries of babies. He followed a nurse into one of the rooms, where he noticed a child about one year old lying in a crib. The baby was covered with horrible bruises, scratches, and scars. At first the pastor thought the child had been in a severe accident. On closer examination, however, he was shocked to see obscenities written in ink all over the child's legs. The baby had been abused. Because of internal injuries, the baby was unable to hold down food. The bottom of his feet were scarred with cigarette burns.

The pastor watched as the nurse reached down to pick up the baby. Tenderly and gently, she lifted the child holding him next to her. The child began to scream, suspect of any kind of human touch. But as she held the baby securely, he slowly began to quiet. Finally, in spite of the wounds, hurts and past experiences, love broke through to the baby's heart. Because of that love, he no longer felt the need to cry.[2]

There are hurting people all around us who have been abused—some physically, but most of them verbally. The son who feels pain and rejection every time his father says, "You can't do anything right," or "Why can't you be like...?" is most likely to flinch if a kind gesture or warm embrace is brought his way. Our sons and daughters need our touch every day. They need to know that they are of great worth in our eyes. They need us to be parents who will risk reaching out and touching them with the love of Christ in ways that can be felt and experienced for a lifetime. Your tenderness will be remembered long after your words fade away.

When we neglect to demonstrate the quality of tenderness as a man, our children are only seeing one side of manhood, and that is inconsistent with what we see in Scripture through God's Son, Jesus Christ. Although He was bold and didn't back down, and even confrontational with the Pharisees, yet He was also tender. He gathered children into His arms, touched the skin of a leper, and spoke words of warmth to the blind. He was rugged yet tender, strong but sensitive, courageous yet caring. We would do well to follow in His steps and point our children in His direction.

Investment/Deposit #3
A DAD TAKES TIME

Over breakfast one morning, a man shared with me that he was making a ton of money. He had just bought a new car, made some great investments, and really enjoyed his career.

I asked him, "And what about your personal investment into your wife and children—where do they fit into the picture?"

He looked at me and said, "I leave before my children are up in the morning, and I come home when my children are in bed. Maybe that's why I feel so lousy when I lay in bed at night and wonder if what I'm doing is truly making me happy."

> No amount of success at the job will compensate for failure at home. To succeed in work but fail at home is to fail completely.[3]

Your children will take to the bank your word of promise that you will spend time with them. But when you fail to fulfill your promise, you are teaching them not to trust you. Trust is extended to the limit of truth and no more. A man shows himself to be trustworthy on the basis of his truthfulness in carrying out, performing, or fulfilling his word. Therefore, when we fail to spend promised time with our children, we neglect our calling as men to not only share with them the way of biblical manhood, but we neglect in showing them the way as well. As one man in our church shared, "His presents from a business trip will never replace the gift of his time."

My father is a true man. He always made time for me. He'd no sooner get out of the car after work, and I'd be standing there with my ball and glove ready to play catch. He'd quickly go inside, kiss mom, share his day, and out he came in his work socks to toss the baseball around before dinner. Hour upon hour of throwing and talking deposited fond memories for a lifetime.

You can't bottle the time spent with them. You need to use it today, because tomorrow it won't be there. It may be getting down on all fours to play horse with your 4-year-old daughter or sledding down Cadillac hill for the first time with your son. Whatever the event, create fond memories for tomorrow with the time you spend with your children today. I'm reminded daily, as I see the years with my wife and kids fly by, that I can't hug them enough, I can't kiss them enough. So when you feel like a full-time taxi service rather than a father or husband, remember it's the tenderness and touch they give you in return that makes it all worthwhile. Future generations will be told about the Lord (Psalm 22:30). Your touch and tenderness to your family will be handed down from generation to generation as He looks in on your home.

But You, O Lord, shall endure forever, and the remembrance of Your name to all generations (Psalm 102:12 NKJV).

The way you treat your family is directly proportionate to the way you treat God.

I was reminded recently of the importance of investing time and togetherness with my children as I came across a story by a pastor:

My eleven year old son and I went for a bike ride last summer to the back roads of central Oregon. I mounted my slick Japanese road bike, he with his department store mountain bike. He had scratched and saved with his paper route earnings for months and he bought it with his own money. We dreamed of this ride through a long Portland winter. Now that we were finally out and together I almost ruined it. He was going so slow! I wanted to fly down those country roads—his shifters weren't working right and every time he tried to downshift or upshift he slowed to a crawl. His de-railer rattled like a Tommy gun. I got so impatient with him. I berated him for his slowness. I said he could do a lot better if he tried. He was spoiling our bike ride. "I'm trying my best," he said.

His new bike just wasn't working very well. We stopped together under the pine trees...sun shining...and I watch him. Head bowed, tears rolling down his cheeks. I felt like a wretch. I embraced him and told him I was sorry for my foolish impatience. Now if my heart was moved to evil as I am by my own son's limitations—how does my heavenly Father feel when I can't keep up and my gears get jammed and my legs get tired. What does He think about me when my dreams fall short or I push myself to the limits—I stop by the side of the road—and I weep and I cry? Does He stay on His bike and say, "Too bad, kid, your legs are too short to bike with God." No! He climbs off, puts His arms around me and He says, "I'll never leave you behind, son. It doesn't matter how far we go because being with you on this bike ride is all that really matters." It doesn't matter how far we go. It just matters that we go together. It doesn't matter all that we accomplish—it just matters that we do accomplish for His glory what He's asked us to do. When I sit in my living room on my couch and I am in tears and I'm wondering, God—are you gonna do it? He reminds me that just being with Him is all that matters.[4]

Investment/Deposit #4
DADS NEED TO PASS THE TORCH

I'm reminded over the years, as I've watched the opening ceremonies of the Summer and Winter Olympic games, of the excitement and anticipation within the stadium when the runner comes through the tunnel holding the lit torch. The runner jogs around the track once and then hands the torch off to another individual who runs up a series of stairs until he's high above the crowd. There, he stretches out his arm with the torch ablaze and lights the Olympic flame, signifying the beginning of the Olympic Games. That flame continues to burn bright throughout the games for all to see. It sets the pace and tone for the weeks ahead. It's a sign of peace, camaraderie, and common ground for all athletics of every nation to gather. It gives witness to those who pass by that this world event of peace is to be carried on over the years. It is a light of hope and joy and steadiness in a world that is engulfed by darkness and fear and instability.

We pass a torch to our children as well. Not for a game, or an event, but we pass the torch of purity, holiness, integrity, and the Good News of Jesus Christ. We instill in them biblical principles that will burn bright and will be seen by all for years to come. It's a torch that displays the blessed hope, the Prince of Peace, the fellowship of believers. It's a torch that sets us apart from the darkened world as we know it. It's a torch that pursues more than gold, silver, or bronze—its goals are holiness, boldness, and perseverance as the race is run for the One who sits on high and sees our every deed.

Our sons and daughters are a witness to others of a blessing given to them by you and me. Is there concern in our voices as we send our children out into a darkened world? You bet! "Did I do all I could?" "Did I cover all my bases with them?" "Did I teach them everything to live a life of godliness?" "Did I do my very best?" These are all questions that plague our soul as we watch them head out on their own. But as they go, we can have the assurance of sending them out with the glowing torch of a godly heritage which will light their way on the path they walk (Psalms 78:5-7). It's the best investment we can ever make, and the dividends are out of this world.

How can we create an atmosphere in our homes where there is more building up than tearing down, more peace than potential problems, more support than sarcasm? It starts by building from the following examples:

• HONOR one another: "Be devoted to one another in brotherly love. Honor one another above yourself" (Romans 12:10).
• SUBMIT to one another: "Submit to one another out of reverence for Christ" (Ephesians 5:21).
• SERVE one another: "Serve wholeheartedly, as if you were serving the Lord, not men" (Ephesians 6:7).
• ENCOURAGE one another: "See to it, brothers, that none of you has a sinful, unbelieving heart that turns away from the living God. But encourage one another daily, as long as it is called Today, so that none of you may be hardened by sin's deceitfulness" (Hebrews 3:12-13).
• CONFESS AND PRAY for one another: "Therefore confess your sins to each other and pray for each other so that you may be healed. The prayer of a righteous man is powerful and effective" (James 5:16).

• LOVE one another: "This is love: not that we loved God, but that He loved us and sent His Son as an atoning sacrifice for our sins. Dear friends, since God so loved us, we ought to love one another" (1 John 4:10-11).

CHARTING YOUR COURSE

SELF-EVALUATION

1. What fond memories do you have of your father in the past or present that you have collected as portraits in your mind and heart?

2. In what ways are you instilling into your children a godly heritage which will light the way on the path they walk?

3. What memories are you creating for your children that will outlive you?

4. What character and temperament do you express to your family when you dock your vessel at the end of each day and walk into the house? How does that affect the atmosphere of the home?

5. Looking back over the chapter, what investment/deposit do you need to take a closer look at in developing a healthier relationship with your children?

6. Are you building up or tearing down your family? Of the 5 building blocks mentioned, which ones do you need to do a better job of laying for your family structure?

GROUP DISCUSSION

1. Look up Deuteronomy 6:4-9; Psalm 112:1-6; 127:1; Ephesians 6:1-4. How do these verses reflect the kind of internal and external boundaries we are to impress upon our children?

Music Resources: "Slow Down" by Michael James, *Shoulder to the Wind* CD

"I Want to be Just Like You" by Phillips, Craig and Dean, *Where the Strength Begins* CD

Sources

[1] Charles Nordhoff and James Norman Hall, *Mutiny on the Bounty* (Little Brown & Co. 1989).

[2] Timothy Wright, *A Community of Joy* (Abingdon Publishing), p.24.

[3] Patrick Morley, *The Seven Seasons of a Man's Life* (Thomas Nelson Publisher, Tennessee 1995), p.61.

[4] *Discipleship Journal* (Navigators), Issue #36, 1986.

Chapter 16
WHO'S AT THE HELM?

Anyone can hold the helm when the sea is calm.
-Unknown

Most of us don't have any idea of how many rules that captains must follow. But the next time you get down near the water, check out how many buoys, lights, and channel markers they must observe and obey along the way. Those markers are placed within view to ensure the safety of all the boats plying the waters, keeping them from hitting another boat or running aground on sandbars.

And so it is in our marriages. When couples first get married, most of them are sensitive to the marriage signs. They say,

> To have and to hold, from this day forward, for better for worse, for richer for poorer, in sickness and in health, to love and to cherish, till death do us part.

There is great excitement, and the road ahead is filled with great possibilities. We don't want to drift asleep, or neglect the instructions that assure a successful marriage, so we pay attention and start out the marriage by faithfully observing all the signs. As the years fly by, however, many become uncomfortable or bored with the road they're on. Often, signs that were obeyed to the nth degree in the beginning have now become disregarded due to the rapid pace of life. We tend to set new standards, and making up our own signs becomes very tempting.

Often in marriages the "I do" at the wedding ceremony later changes to "No, I won't;" and the original openness toward intimacy is transformed into signs of isolation. Careless marriage partners, like careless captains, find themselves disregarding the other and traveling on the way of relationships without any concern for the one who is nearest to them. Jeremiah 6:16 speaks of the signs of the times:

> *This is what the Lord says: Stand at the crossroads and look; ask for the ancient paths* [sign posts], *ask where the good way is, and walk in it, and you will find rest for your souls* (NIV).

Many spouses are finding themselves at a fork in the river, relaxing down in the cabin, wondering who will take the initiative and go up topside to take control of the helm of their home and marriage and navigate it down the right course. We men must take that God-given initiative! We must navigate our wife and children through every storm, every sunrise, and every sunset for the long haul. Being an effective husband and father is a full-time job. We are to be the family's protector, provider, lover, and friend. To do otherwise is to let our families drift down the wrong fork where the enemy awaits to move in and destroy. Too often we neglect the task of steering our marriage on a steady course of respect, love, and understanding. Instead we become slack and, whether consciously or ignorantly, let the marriage aimlessly head on a collision course with a sandbar that spells disaster to our hull. What we must be are faithful men who are willing to grasp the helm of our marriage and home and be a spiritual guide, beloved husband, and masculine father. We need helmsmen who remain steady during the storms of life and show tenderness when they know it's needed.

SIGNS OF THE TIMES

Here are a few signs couples display as they journey through life. Are any of them becoming more apparent in your marriage? If they are, now is the time as a helmsmen to steer your marriage and family in a new direction.

NO TRESPASSING/DO NOT ENTER: Paul and Michelle have faced several difficult problems in their 18 years of marriage. Many would consider them the model married couple; but under the surface, Paul and Michelle have for years subtly pushed each other out of their own "personal areas." They have not been completely open with each other because of past hurts which have not been resolved and restored. They have, therefore, declared certain areas "off limits." Their trust in each other has diminished, resulting in isolation and personal detachment as the hull of their hearts become hardened.

BEWARE OF DOG: Diane and Randy are constantly critical of each other and of others in general. When invited over to their house, others feel tension, especially when one of the two lashes out with barks of criticism toward their spouse. Criticism is like an unknown dog—you don't know whether to trust the dog or run from it, for it can turn on you in an instant. And so it is with some couples, where there is more criticism than encouragement, and praise is replaced by belittling. The result is a family whose members walk around the house on egg shells, not knowing what's going to happen next.

DIVIDED HIGHWAY: Tony Campolo describes one marriage this way, "He liked to walk alone; she liked to walk alone; they got married; they walked alone together." In other words, he had his priorities; she had hers—different goals, different dreams, different lives. It's a sign of a divided marriage. Sadly, it's often the children who suffer the most. They get tossed to and fro, not having a clear understanding of where the family is headed because mom and dad are doing their own thing. It's no wonder that when the children get old they begin to do their own thing. They are just imitating the very actions they have seen for so many years from mom and dad.

Statistics show that in the first year of marriage couples will communicate 70 minutes a day; they communicate 30 minutes a day the second year, 15 minutes a day the third year, 10 minutes a day the fourth year, and by the tenth year of marriage only five minutes a day. Let's be careful that lack of communication and mixed priorities do not divide our marriages.

Now, let me offer three signs that when observed and obeyed will enable a helmsmen to navigate his wife and family to safe passage.

SOFT SHOULDER: Can your wife and children come to you for emotional, physical, and spiritual support? Can they lean on your shoulder to find comfort, encouragement, and love? Often instead of offering a soft shoulder of love, we offer a cold shoulder of resentment, unrealistic demands, or outright belittling of the individual. May our days and nights be filled with the comfort and affection of a binding love. Don't let the troubles and trials of life intrude upon the coziness of a night spent in the arms of your beloved. Men, let's wear a "Soft Shoulder" sign for our wife and kids.

CHILDREN PLAYING: Cindy and Dave have been married for 23 years, but you would think they were honeymooners by the fun and laughter they share with their children and each other. Does your family consist of more laughter and "playing" than sadness and turmoil? May our families carry with them the words of Psalm 126:2, "Our mouths were filled with laughter, our tongues with songs of joy."

YIELD: This sign tells us to slow down and wait till oncoming traffic moves on before we can ease out. Likewise, in our marriage, if we are not willing to yield, submit, and take the role of servant as well as helmsman in our homes, we will eventually shipwreck our life and take our family down with us. You see, true love doesn't worry about who's the boss. It doesn't keep score in the "whose turn is it now" game. True love rejoices and is willing to yield in doing what is good for the joy of serving one another.

But he that is greatest among you shall be your servant (Matthew 23:11).

AVOIDING COLLISION

A faithful helmsmen who seeks to guide his wife and children through the seas of life is conscious of avoiding certain situations that can and will bring internal and external damage to those closest to him. His ability to maintain a steady course avoiding the reefs filled with danger is crucial. Here are several factors that must be considered.

1. *Keep a proper balance as protector, provider, lover, and friend.* I've seen helmsmen who are great providers but lousy lovers or excellent

protectors who fail miserably as a beloved friend. A proper balance must be maintained between the four. When one of the four is emphasized more than the other, we rob our family of experiencing the wholeness of biblical masculinity. We need to demonstrate the role of:

Protector—We should protect our wife and children in the same manner that our Lord protects us:
• He protects us by teaching us discernment—Proverbs 2:11.
• He protects us from the enemy and his influences—Deuteronomy 23:14; Psalms 12:5-7; John 17:15.
• He protects us from trouble—Psalm 32:7.
• He protects us by instilling godly wisdom—Proverbs 3-4.
• He protects us with love and truth—Psalm 25:21; 40:11.
• He protects our eyes from harmful influences and impurity—Habakkuk 1:13; Ephesians 5:3-4; 1 Thessalonians 4:3-8.

Provider—There are numerous ways which we are to provide in our marriage, but the one element that immediately comes to mind is providing financial stability. Scripture is clear on how we are to provide for our family.

> *If anyone does not provide for his relatives, and especially for his immediate family, he has denied the faith and is worse than an unbeliever* (1 Timothy 5:8).

To be a faithful provider for the home is crucial in the modeling process of godly character.

Lover—Do you go on dates? Do you demonstrate touch in your marriage? Holding hands, touching the skin, a kiss on the lips, the commitment to serve, and sexual harmony are all signs of a healthy marriage. The question should not be, "Do you love your wife?," but "Are you her lover?" Anyone can say they love their spouse, and yet be miles apart in intimacy, respect, communication, and romantic harmony. When you can say with assuredness that you are your wife's lover, you immediately visualize acts of love that have been demonstrated in the past and will continue in the future. The Song of Solomon paints a wonderful picture of Solomon as a lover:

> *Let him kiss me with the kisses of his mouth, for your love is more delightful than wine (1:2).*

How handsome you are, my lover! Oh, how charming! And our bed is verdant (1:16).
Like an apple tree among the trees of the forest so is my lover among the young men.
I delight to sit in his shade, and his fruit is sweet to my taste (2:3).
My lover is mine and I am his (2:16; 6:3; 7:10).
How beautiful you are, my darling! Oh how beautiful! Your eyes behind your veil are doves (4:1).
His mouth is sweetness itself; he is altogether lovely. This is my lover, this my friend (5:16).
Let us be able to say as Solomon said, "I am my lover's and my lover is mine" (6:3).

Friend—You and your mate should be closest of friends. That's a good example for your children to see being lived out before them. My wife truly is my best friend. And as best friends we share, care, love, and help each other as only best friends can. We enjoy the company of one another and seek through our conversation and activities together to grow in the richness of our marriage. The bride in the Song of Solomon said of her husband, "This is my beloved, and this is my friend" (5:16). Our role as husbands is not to distance ourselves from our mate, but to display the same friendship that Christ Jesus displays to us on a daily basis.

2. *Maintain order when an offense or conflict arises.* Comments like, "She will get over it; she always does," or, "My kids can deal with it; they have broad shoulders," are signs of insensitivity to our family's needs. Not dealing with an offense or conflict within the home, or making light of it, can bring bitterness, resentment and even hatred. I don't know about you, but when there is conflict in our home, or something has brought tension and restlessness in place of peace, I cannot rest until we talk about it and try to get it resolved. We will assassinate our relationships by sweeping conflict under the rug.

We must understand that a woman's makeup is extremely different from that of a man's. Both are wonderful, but there is a great difference. A woman is like a ship with every compartment of the ship open: everything flows from one thing to another. Feelings, therefore, that are involved, filter down through everything that happens throughout the day. Men can shut off one compartment and go on to another, not realizing that something is still gnawing at the hull of our family's heart and is beginning to break up our crew members' self-worth.

During times of conflict and misunderstanding, we need to keep a clear head. We must not panic or make rash decisions; we must not throw caution to the wind or put our family in jeopardy. A faithful helmsman knows how to weather the storms that occur both *within* the home and *outside* of it. He learns to react, but not overreact. He demonstrates wisdom, not foolishness, and he seeks the interests of others rather than carrying out his own agenda (Philippians 2:3-4).

3. *The ability to apologize when you've blown it:* There is a tendency in our masculine nature to excuse, justify, and place the blame on others before we'll humbly say those three significant words to our loved ones: I AM SORRY. The conversation may go something like this:

Wife: Can't you for once just say you're sorry?
Husband: OK, "you're" sorry. *Or...*

Wife: It would mean the world to me if you would say you were sorry.
Husband: Why should I say it, when I don't mean it anyway. *Or...*

Wife: Why do your "I'm sorry's" precede a huge but?
Husband: I wasn't aware of that, let's talk about your huge butt!

Those are pretty harsh words coming from a man who is to be standing at the helm of his vessel with his wife and children clinging to him for love and support. I have found over the years in my marriage with Ann that the best way to get the last word in (that's what we really want anyway, isn't it?) is to apologize. Pride is usually what keeps most of us from telling those around us that we're sorry, that we were wrong, that we blew it. Pride is wicked and crafty, because it's hard to see or grasp. But when it shows up, you know it's there because it will try to invade your home and stand in the way of forgiveness taking place between two parties. Asking forgiveness and saying we're sorry shows we're willing to humble ourselves and make changes in our life for the betterment of our family. To say we're sorry and yet not work on what we're sorry for makes for a difficult time for the family. We build love and trust in our family toward us when we make the necessary corrective actions in our life following our apologies.

4. *Maintain eye contact.* "We don't look at each other anymore," she said. "I'm afraid to look in his eyes. My fear is that he's hiding something from me, and I'm afraid of what that might be." Are you hiding something from your wife and kids that you fear if they find out, it might destroy your family? I assure you, by not looking into their eyes they will become suspicious even if you're not hiding anything from them. If you can't look your wife and kids in the eyes, then the trust factor may be in question. There may be a loss of interest/intimacy, or even a sense of guilt for not fulfilling our responsibility as husband and father. The coldness our family will feel when we neglect to look at them, honor them, and compliment them will freeze them from eventually being able to show that to others. Determine today to look into your family's eyes and into the eyes of God with a clear conscience.

Men, this voyage we are on is too important to mess up. We must follow the right signs if we intend to navigate our family toward the closeness and intimacy that Christ desires for every home.

AM I MAKING THE GRADE?

When a man comes to grips with his responsibility of taking the role of helmsman in his home, he's not afraid or defensive when he asks his wife or children how he's doing. From time to time, I will ask my wife and children how I'm doing as a husband and a dad in a number of areas. They are always honest with me (sometimes too honest), which enables me to evaluate my effectiveness in the family. Below is a resource that I have found to be very helpful in determining the progress I'm making in my marriage. Make two copies—one for yourself and one for your wife. Men, use the following grades to help you evaluate the health of your marriage. Have your wife evaluate you on the same basis. When you're finished, compare yours with hers and discuss areas that are strong and areas that can be improved. One word of caution. Be open and sensitive to each other's reasoning for the grade given. The goal through this exercise is to enhance your marriage, not cause friction.

Use the following grades to determine the health of your marriage:
A= Outstanding B= Good C= Average D= Poor F= Don't even ask
1. _____Helps around the house without being asked.
2. _____Prays with me at least once a week (excluding meals).
3. _____Prays for me, and asks how he can pray for me.
4. _____Helps with the children (baths, bedtime, mealtime,
        taxi driver to and from activities).
5. _____Demonstrates a spirit of leadership in wise decision making.
6. _____Listens, asks questions, and cares about my day.
7. _____Tells me he loves me.

Shows love for me in the following ways:
8. _____Verbal expression (praise, compliments, affirmation).
9. _____Notes of encouragement or gifts of praise.
10. _____Gives me undivided attention.
11. _____Is tender and gentle in showing affection on a regular basis
        (i.e., hand holding, hugs, kisses, etc.).
12. _____Acts of service (i.e projects that need done).
13. _____Takes initiative in making sure we get to church
        and involved within the body of Christ.
14. _____Is interested in my spiritual walk with Christ.
15. _____Is truthful with me in his financial, spiritual, and social life.

➤ CHARTING YOUR COURSE ➤

SELF-EVALUATION
1. How much eye contact do you think you make with your wife in a day?   1 hour or more?   1/2 hour to an hour?
        10 minutes to a 1/2 hour?   Less than ten minutes?

2. What do eye contact and intimacy have in common?

3. As a helmsmen, in what ways do you demonstrate to your family a proper balance as: A. Protector? B. Provider? C. Lover? D. Friend?
4. After answering "Am I Making the Grade," what conclusions did you come to regarding the kind of helmsman you are in your family?

5. What needs to be improved?

GROUP DISCUSSION

1. Why is it so hard for many men to tell their wife or children "I am sorry?"

2. When an offense or conflict arises in your home, what should be done?

3. Make a list of ways that you can demonstrate honor and appreciation for your spouse this next week. Then pick one or two out and make a commitment to follow through on them.

Video Resources:

Making The Most Of Your Marriage (4 volumes) by John Maxwell of Injoy Ministries (1-800-333-6506).

Love For A LifeTime by David T. Moore, Senior Pastor at Southwest Community Church in La Quinta, California. www.mooreonlife.com.

Music Resources:

"Ordinary Life" by Chad Brock, *Chad Brock* CD, 1998 McSpadden Music.

"I See Jesus in You" by Reba Rambo and Dony McGuire, 1986 New Kingdom Music.

COORDINATE #7

Navigating
Through
the Storms of Life

Chapter 17

STORMS ON THE HORIZON

I am not afraid of storms, for I am learning how to sail my ship.
—Louisa May Alcott

It was to be a joyous Friday evening as Pastor Riggs was making his way to the church. In less than an hour, the future bride and groom would be arriving with friends and family for a wedding rehearsal before the actual ceremony Saturday afternoon. As usual, Pastor Riggs decided to arrive early at church to open up and tie up any loose ends for the wedding and Sunday's sermon. But for Pastor Riggs the evening would be anything but joyous and exciting. It would become an evening of unforgettable pain and tragedy. A single cloud appears on the horizon.

As the pastor pulled into the church parking lot, he heard what sounded like a plastic milk jug being run over under his car. As he looked out the rearview mirror, he was shocked to see a little body lying on the ground. Quickly he jumped out of the car, ran over, and bent down to where four-year-old Matthew was lying in great pain. Looking up, he saw some people who were congregating near the church entrance and yelled for them to call 911 immediately.

A CLUSTER OF CLOUDS

Little Matthew, who lived next door to the church, had been playing baseball in the parking lot and was running to get his ball when he ran out in front of Pastor Riggs' car. "I didn't even see him," Riggs said. The vision of a plastic bat bent and broken would be a reminder of the heartache and pain which Riggs would undergo over the next few months. Matthew was rushed to the hospital. "It was a life and death situation," said Riggs. "I prayed, 'Please Lord, don't let this little boy die; take my life instead. I've lived a full life. Let him live; he's only four years old.'"

Matthew made it to the hospital alive that night, but died a short time later. No amount of comforting, words of encouragement, or prayer could at that moment take away the dagger of pain, guilt, and sorrow that Pastor Riggs was experiencing over the loss of this child. It would be months before the pastor would again see the sunlight of restoration, hope, and joy that had been covered by the raging storm of that Friday evening tragedy.

How do you respond and what do you hang onto as an anchor when the scene changes without warning, when the winds of passion suddenly die, or the clouds of despair lurk on the horizon? I love the quote by Adlard Coles in his book, *Heavy Weather Sailing*. It proves to be an excellent analogy of the storms we face from time to time:

> Gales are rarely pleasant experiences, except for the sense of exhilaration in their early stages, and of elation when they have passed. The intermediate part is often one of anxiety and tiredness, but, whether one likes it or not heavy weather at some time or another is the lot of most of us.

We've all faced storms and know others who have faced them as well. Some storms are bigger than others. And the thought of them may still bring a chill to the bones. Memories of a painful ordeal stir the emotions, often leaving the soul and spirit crippled and confused for years to come. Here are a few of those clouds that can make their way into our arena.

- an unexpected job transfer
- the loss of a job
- an emergency call at midnight
- financial problems
- the adoption falls through
- a church split
- divorce papers from your spouse
- the death of a loved one
- a miscarriage
- your spouse is having an affair
- hearing the words, "it's cancer"
- spiritual or physical burnout

MIND GAMES

During times of guilt, tragedy, and failure we often resort to the ruthless mind game called "if only." We bargain with God, begging and pleading with Him to wake us up from this living nightmare we're in. We tell Him we'll do anything, become anything, or go anywhere if only He removes us from the current state we're in.

When there is no immediate answer or relief from the raging storm, we begin the process of beating ourselves up by playing the "if only" game. *If only* I could have avoided this. . . I would have listened. . .I knew sooner. . . I had been there. . . *If only, if only, if only,* echoes down the corridors of our minds.

It is here the enemy loves to slide in whispering questions and accusations that rip and wreak havoc on the soul and spirit: "There must be sin in my life." "And I call myself a Christian." "God is punishing me." "I sure have blown it." "Things were so much easier before I knew Christ." "I might as well give up and let the storm consume me."

Many are the cries of those who have been taken captive by the storms of life that try to knock the confidence, passion, and drive to continue out of many of us. Fear and doubt quickly flood in, causing many of us to poorly handle the present storm, thus navigating our lives in a direction contrary to the coordinates of God's intentions. We react in many ways that do not acknowledge our faith in God.

ISOLATION: "I just shut down and become numb to the situation. I retreat into my dark cave and do not want to be bothered." Comments like these often surface when we are hit hard by a squall that was unexpected or unavoidable. Often our reasoning is that the more we can isolate our feelings and thoughts from the pain, the quicker we'll get over it and can move on. Isolation, however, is an illusion which the enemy will use to work against us in our weakened condition.

We think by avoiding or burying our pain, it will in some way disappear. The problem is that when we choose to isolate our feelings, we are often launched into a state of depression, hindering the soul from being revived and built back up. We become *prisoners* of the tragedy, thus it becomes our master, fueling every thought and intention of the heart in an unhealthy way. We tell others, "I don't want to think about it or talk about it." And yet that is exactly what we need to begin doing. Restoration and freedom cannot result when we choose to isolate and bury our pain. Somewhere along the way it must be resurrected, verbalized, and dealt with so we can move on toward personal confidence and spiritual wholeness of the inner soul.

LASHING OUT: Statements like, "Nobody understands the pain, confusion and heartache I bear," come to the surface when we initially begin to express feelings. There may be few answers to the many questions that plague the soul. We tend to take it out on those who love us most—our wife, children, or a friend who doesn't understand what we are going through. We may even lash out at God. Infuriated responses like, "Is this some kind of joke?" or "So this is how you treat Your children!" often occur under the pressure of dealing with life's disappointments and pain. In time we begin to realize how foolish these tactics are. Instead we need to reach out as we let the indwelling Spirit of the living God be our comforter and encourager in our deepest anguish.

> *The righteous cry out, and the Lord hears them; He delivers them from their troubles. The Lord is close to the brokenhearted and saves those who are crushed in spirit* (Psalms 34:17-18).

> *He heals the brokenhearted and binds up their wounds* (Psalm 147:3).

REBELLION: When the storm is rolling in and it seems like all hell is breaking loose around us, there is the tendency and temptation to want to abandon anything or anyone who reminds us of our present situation. The attraction is to *run from* the problem or pain rather than *face it*. It is in this rebellious condition that we tend to revert back to childish behavior. Most of us can remember playing hide and seek as a child. We would wait till it was dark, having a place in mind that we had strategically scouted out earlier in the day so when the time came to play we could quickly run to our spot and hide, hoping no one would find us and reveal our hiding place. It's cute for a child to play hide and seek. But when a man plays hide and seek, skirting responsibilities, it's not cute any more.

There are many forms of hiding that men use to deal with the situation at hand: prayerlessness; diving into our work to numb the pain; neglecting to go home and deal with a conflict that has escalated; not being in the Word; little or no involvement in church; seeking our own self interests by consuming alcohol, pornography, etc. All of these tactics are means whereby a man will avoid dealing with death, disappointment, trials, or guilt that enters into his world.

STAYING BUSY: Burying ourselves in our work, or a project, is a tactic we will often revert to, in order to distract us from memories of a painful incident of the past. We become so engrossed in our busyness that when it comes time to sleep, our bodies are so exhausted that we immediately sleep rather than give our minds a chance to think or reason. In the process, however, as we maintain an endless flow of busyness, we eventually burn ourselves out. We cause more harm to our body and emotions than we would by coming to grips with the reality that we must address and heal from the hurts and guilt of our past.

A great example of this is found in the life of the Apostle Peter. After denying the Lord, Peter went back and occupied his time and attention on what he could do best—fishing. He didn't want to be reminded of how he had let the Lord down and ran away when he should have taken a stand. Peter doesn't seem to deal with it until he is sitting with Christ (John 21:1-19) next to a warm fire after having just jumped into the Sea of Tiberias. We do not see Christ reprimand him over his lack of loyalty, but instead we see Christ lovingly begin to heal the past wounds by giving him new memories to hold onto. To hear Christ tell Peter three times to feed his sheep must have lifted the heavy load that Peter had been carrying around. It brought hope, restoration, and a revived spirit to Peter's struggling soul. The closure that Peter experienced, having finally faced what he was running from, must have brought a smile to his face as he breathed a sigh of relief. Freedom and peace were ushered in. He had no more haunted past; he didn't need to beat himself up any more. The welcoming words of Christ in verse 19 saying "Follow Me," must have put a passion and vibrancy back into the sails of Peter's faith. He was released to live, love, and laugh as he went forth turning the world upside down for the cause of Christ.

ANCHOR POINTS FOR THE HURTING SOUL

This world is like a sea—restless, ruthless, and at times dangerous. It is never at a standstill, so finding true stability is a rare thing. Human affairs and dilemmas may be compared to waves driven into the port side of our lives, making us feel thrown about. We are likely to get bruised along the way, carried off by strong currents of influence, driven off course by winds of despair, and tossed by some of the most horrendous of storms along the way. Yet we must not forget that this is not our home; we have not yet come to the mainland, which in our metaphor is our eternal resting place of glory for the people of God. In the meantime, there will be squalls of sorrow and thunderous trials, but we must never forget that He has been pleased to weld an anchor of hope for us that is very sure and steadfast, so that we may withstand the storm and continue on the course after it's over.

The next crucial question is: How does a person heal from the storms of disappointment and pain? Over the years, I've found there's no easy answer to that question. Each person and each situation is unique. I have spoken to hundreds of people over the years whose lives have been ripped apart due to life's trials and turmoil. Are we to assume then that over a period of time these individuals just got used to the pain? Did they in some way endure or adjust to it, concocting a carefree mentality that everything was fine and life could now be lived once again through rose colored glasses? We're ignorant if we think such a thing. We hurt, we cry, we play the mind games even years after the incident occurred. Sure, sometimes we forget, but most of the time we never fully recover from the crushing blow it had on our life. What we need is restoration of not only the soul, but of our own personal confidence that through the pain we're still useful, valuable, and we feel assured that something good will come out of all this heartache. It's in those darkened times that we desperately need someone who will be an anchor to grab onto when the storms of life come rolling in.

In the process of finding answers, I began surveying people who have lost loved ones or been through a personal crisis and have experienced gut wrenching pain and heartache in life. Though each situation is different, I asked individuals what they held onto during those times that became an anchor point for them in their personal healing. The following are some anchor points that have been a source of stability and strength for many along the way.

Anchor Point #1:
HOLD FIRM TO THE PROMISES OF GOD

During times of uncertainty we must remember to focus on those things which breathe life into the soul. Like an anchor, the promises of God are needed to keep us from losing the headway we have made up to this point.

As Charles Spurgeon so aptly put it,

> Suppose a ship is making good progress toward its intended port but the wind changes and blows directly at it. The vessel is in danger of being carried back to the port from which it started, or to an equally undesirable port. In order to resist the turbulent wind, it must put down its anchor.[1]

Likewise, believers are sometimes tempted to return to the old ways from which they once came, saying life as a Christian is too difficult, too demanding, and too much of a discomfort. We are inclined to renounce the things that we've learned and to conclude that they never have been reliable or dependable. Our old sinful nature and the craftiness of the devil grabs hold of us and tries to pull us back. If we did not have the anchor of His promises to secure our hold in troubled times, reassuring us that the storm will indeed cease, many of us would let go of Him and head back. Let's not lose sight of the wonderful promises of God; let's not give the enemy and our flesh a foothold to deceive and drive us back.

Here are a few promises that, as His children, we need to keep close to our heart:

- I will not fail you - Joshua 1:5.
- I will guide you - Psalm 32:8.
- I will deliver you - Psalm 50:15.
- I will strengthen you - Isaiah 41:10.
- I will uphold you - Isaiah 41:10.
- I will comfort you - Isaiah 66:13.
- I will forgive you - Jeremiah 31:34.
- I will restore you - Jeremiah 30:17.

Anchor Point #2:
BEGIN RECALLING FOND MEMORIES

It's during times of confusion, frustration, and grief that we need to recall the memories of the past so they may help heal the wounds of the present (Philippians 3:1-21; 1 Thessalonians 3:6; 2 Peter 1:12-15). We need to cling to something tangible when life and purpose seems to be slipping away. What positive memories can you meditate on that will put purpose, life, and direction back into your sail once again? Here are a few possible ones for you to think about:

- the birth of your son or daughter
- a men's conference where God spoke to your heart in a tender way
- making the winning shot in a live or die championship game
- your wife becomes pregnant
- your child says, "Daddy" for the first time
- a good day at work
- your teenager comes home instead of going to a questionable party
- a friend says the right thing at just the right time
- accomplishing a long term goal
- when your wife gives you a card that says you're the best
- when Christ answers a personal prayer request
- when your worship is fresh and real with your heavenly Father
- when your kids say, "You're the man, Dad."
- you shared your faith with a friend, neighbor, or co-worker
- when you kept going and didn't give in the day you got saved
- special vacations and holidays as a family
- when your Dad or Mom voiced how proud they were of you

Anchor Point #3
SEEK OUT THE COUNSEL AND
ENCOURAGEMENT OF CLOSE FRIENDS

We need the care and support of those who know us best during critical times. They may not be able to answer every question regarding what we are going through, but like a friend told me later after I sat with him while his newborn was on the edge of life and death, "It was just having you there that mattered more than what you shared." Those in your church, a body of believers from another church, a co-worker, or a close network of friends are needed in assuring the troubled individual of Christ's love, forgiveness, and comfort.

Anchor Point #4
LEAN ON THE SHOULDER OF YOUR WIFE

Statements like, "Their presence not only brought comfort, but it drew us closer together," and "She sat and cried with me rather than letting me wallow in my own misery, and I grew to love her even more from that moment on," are encouraging responses from those whose hearts were lifted because of a sympathetic and understanding wife. When our wife is experiencing heartache in a way that does not affect us, we have the choice of entering into her situation and feeling her pain, or becoming distant and unattached to her sorrow. The one will build bridges of love and loyalty for a lifetime, and the other will slowly burn any bridges that had been built up to that point. Make the right choice and enter her pain.

Anchor Point #5
IMMERSE YOURSELF IN HIS WORD

Cling to the resurrection. If Christ can be resurrected from the dead, He is powerful enough to resurrect you from your present situation and restore you back to purposeful living once again. Comments like these are always encouraging to hear: "I let the Word heal the weeping soul. I lived in it, I camped out in His Word." "You have got to do what you have to do, because you know you're His. He is the one who heals the brokenhearted. Out of the bitter comes the sweet." "I held to His Word like a child clings to his pacifier. It was a necessity." Others have shared that they began reading literature and biographies of those who had undergone suffering and pain, and how they were able to look past the cloud to the change it would have on their life for the glory of the Father.

To those who are presently in the middle of a storm—don't let the storm consume you, but learn all you can through this time. If you can get a sense of what is happening, you will be less likely to be taken by surprise the next time the clouds appear on the horizon. Be encouraged, brother. Here you are today, protected by His grace, provisioned by His mercy, steered by heavenly wisdom, and propelled by the Spirit's power. Thanks to the anchor, or rather to the God who gave it to you, no storm has overwhelmed you. Your life is underway for the port of glory.

> Hallelujah! I believe! Now the giddy world stands fast,
> For my soul has found an anchor till the night of storm is past.[2]

CHARTING YOUR COURSE

SELF-EVALUATION

1. God promises to be with us and comfort us in our pain. In what ways have you sensed His presence and comfort in your life during times of great pain and suffering?

2. What are some fond memories you can dwell on as an anchor for your soul when the clouds of sorrow and turmoil come your way?

3. Are there any storms similar to Pastor Riggs' that you have experienced in the past? How have they affected you positively or negatively?

4. Have you found yourself ever bargaining, begging, or pleading with the Lord to get you out of a current storm you are in? Why?

5. From time to time we tend to play the ruthless mind game of "if only." Have you ever played this game? How did the enemy get a foothold in your thinking as you were in the heat of the storm? (See Ephesians 4:27; 6:10-20.)

GROUP DISCUSSION

1. What do you typically do when you find yourself in a storm and there seems to be no clearing out on the horizon?

2. Are there any other anchor points that can be used?

Video Resource:
Edge T.V. Edition 24- *Doubt*. A gripping video of a youth pastor who loses his wife, child and job to AIDS. If you have ever wrestled with the storm clouds of doubt or grief, this video will encourage you and

help you to cling to the anchor of God's love and sufficiency. Call to order (1-800-616-EDGE) or write P.O. Box 35005, Colorado Springs, Colorado 80935.

Reading Resource:
Edwin Louis Cole, *Winners Are Not Those Who Never Fail, But Those Who Never Quit* (Honor Books).

Music Resources:
"The Blessing in the Thorn" by Phillips, Craig and Dean, off their *Where Strength Begins* CD.
"The Anchor Holds" by Ray Boltz.

Sources
[1] Spurgeon Charles, *Finding Peace in Life's Storms* (Whitaker House, New Kensington, Pennsylvania 1997), p.41.

[2] *Ibid*, p.41.

Chapter 18
LIFE'S UNDERCURRENTS

If you've ever been in one, you'll never forget it.

I have painful memories of getting smashed to the bottom of the ocean floor while on a missions trip in Puerto Rico. I was trying to body surf and ride the waves as they came into shore. What I was ignorant of at the time was the undercurrent that came with those waves. I felt the strong pull of the ocean water on my legs, but in the excitement of it all, I found myself ignoring the undercurrent which eventually pulled me under as I struggled to find which direction was up. Battered and disoriented, I made my way to the beach were I laid exhausted. I made sure I would be more alert the next time and was quick to inform newcomers walking into the surf that strong undercurrents lay just below the surface.

How about you? What are the undercurrents you face from day to day that if you're not careful and alert will damage the soul, body, and spirit of your walk with Christ and others?

Here are several undercurrents that lay just below the surface of the soul that can pull us under and drown our faith if we are not careful:

- Envy
- Discouragement/Doubt
- Pride
- Prejudice/Judgmental Attitudes

- Fear
- Lust
- Atrophy of Spiritual Vibrance and Leadership

ENVY: I know what you're thinking. I'm not envious. Oh, yeah? What about that college grad who just came into your department at work? You know, the one who got the position you'd been waiting years to get? Or how about your independently wealthy neighbor...the one who has everything handed to him on a silver platter while you're working your tail off to make the mortgage and car payment on time. Maybe envy has even crept into your church because someone was asked to be a deacon and you were passed by. Envy can sneak into our minds unexpectedly like a burglar. It doesn't happen everyday, but when it does, we feel violated and abused in some way. If we're smart, we won't entertain thoughts of envy which in the end will rot the bones. (See Proverbs 14:30.)

DISCOURAGEMENT AND DOUBT: Ever been plagued by self-doubt? Do you beat yourself up with feelings of worthlessness, inferiority or failure to clear the bar of expectations? Do you question if God can ever use the gifts and abilities He bestowed upon you long before the foundations of the world began? Self-doubt has a way of paralyzing our souls. (See John 20:24-29.) Let's dismiss these thoughts and replace them with the promise that our worth and identity lie in Christ. Our identity is not based on performance, by what we possess, or by what we know. Our sufficiency is in a heavenly Father who seeks our best by moving us from: doubt to belief; discouragement to renewed in spirit; reservation to realization.

PRIDE: Pride hangs around and camouflages itself just as effectively as other besetting sins. Pride. . . so crafty. . . so subtle. . . so deadly. It often hides behind a mask of false humility. When truly revealed, its lethal and destructive course can cause the most godly men to rest on their own abilities rather than the guidance and direction of God.

Dr. Gary Rosberg, founder of Cross Trainers Men's Ministries in Des Moines, Iowa, shared with me one day over breakfast, "Pride will kill you. It will get you to focus more on what you could be in the future, rather than what you are right now. It is never satisfied, never content, never quenched, and thrives like a deadly cancer cell to get you to think more highly of yourself than what you really are." (See Romans 12:3.)

Pride lurks just below the surface for many men in corporations and ministries today. It has one assignment—to determine the area(s) in which we can be tempted for selfish gain, and then destroy us with the promise that what we seek will in some way bring lasting peace and purpose for life.

Are you plagued by a prideful spirit? Is there a secret spirit of pride that walks down the corridors of your mind wanting to be exalted, craving the limelight, or secretly questing for the attention of human praise? Is there a secret fondness of wanting to be noticed, recognized, or an inner drive to make a name for yourself? Am I hitting too close to home? Maybe it's the love of drawing attention to yourself in conversational circles, giving the impression that you know more than you really do. Maybe it's the guy across the hall at your office, or the guy at church. Is it your neighbor three doors down who does a great job of covering up his faults in order to leave a better impression about himself than is true? What is it for you? Has pride become an undercurrent in your life? This undercurrent will ruin our opportunity to be used as a mighty vessel for the glory of God. If we seek to have God's hand remain on our shoulder, then resist the temptations to think of yourself as something other than a privileged child of God.

PREJUDICE AND JUDGMENTAL ATTITUDES: "I don't have a prejudiced bone in my body." Ever make that comment? Yet prejudice, racial slurs, and judgmental remarks can come out in a rush before we are even conscience of the fact. It will destroy relationships and put up walls of dissension for years to come. My mother often said to me, and I'm sure yours did, too, "Think before you speak or act." I've learned that lesson over the years, sad to say sometimes the hard way.

The humorous story is told of a Chinese man and a Jewish man who were eating lunch together. Suddenly, without warning, the Jewish man got up, walked over to the Chinese fellow, and punched him in the mouth, sending him sprawling to the floor. The Chinese man picked himself up, rubbed his jaw and asked, "What in the world did you do that for?"

The Jewish man replied, "That was for Pearl Harbor!"

"Pearl Harbor!" cried the Chinese man. "I didn't have anything to do with Pearl Harbor. It was the Japanese who bombed Pearl Harbor."

The Jewish man responded, "Chinese, Japanese, Taiwanese— they're all the same to me."

With that they both sat down again, and before too long the Chinese man got up and walked over to the Jewish man and sent him flying across the room with a solid punch to the jaw.

The Jewish man yelled out, "What did you do that for?"

The Chinese man responded, "That's for the Titanic!"

"The Titanic? Why, I didn't have anything to do with the Titanic!"

Whereupon the Chinese man replied, "Goldberg, Feinberg, iceberg—they're all the same to me."[1]

Let's stop blaming our prejudiced attitudes on generations past and start treating everyone with dignity and respect the way we would choose to be treated. Prejudiced thinking toward race, color, or creed will always be one of the greatest obstacles to progress. Let's think justly rather than critically of others. We never know when they may come to our rescue.

FEAR: It's not the circumstance that threatens to destroy us; it's our own fear about it that does the damage. Numbers 13 is an excellent example of becoming immobilized by fear. God commissioned numerous Israelites to go and check out the land of Canaan to see what it was like. They knew this land was theirs to inherit and possess for the Lord had approved it (vs.1). They were told what to explore and then return with a report of what they found (vs.17-20). Yet when they reported back what the land was like, they (with the exception of Joshua and Caleb) only centered on one aspect of their search—the size of the people who dwelled there.

They gave Moses this account: "We went into the land to which you sent us, and it does flow with milk and honey! Here is its fruit. But the people who live there are powerful, and the cities are fortified and very large. We even saw descendants of Anak there." But the men who had gone up with Joshua and Caleb said, "We can't attack those people; they are stronger than we are." And they spread among the Israelites a bad report about the land they had explored. They said, "The land we explored devours those living in it. All the people we saw there are of great size" (Numbers 13:27-29,31-32).

Fear began to set in, causing them to doubt themselves and the affirmation of God's calling on their lives (vs.27-33). Their perspective shifted from the possible to the impossible, from peace to panic; crippling and paralyzing them from trusting and taking God at His Word. Let's keep in mind when this particular undercurrent rolls in, that perfect love drives out fear (1 John 4:18).

LUST: No sexual misdeed has ever been as great as the pain, regret, and consequences it causes later. Yet many men fall into the undercurrent of lust and never get out. Don't fall for the ploy that has smashed many lives on the rock bottom of instant gratification.

Neil Anderson in his book, *Victory Over the Darkness,* shows how easily we can get swept under by rationalizing the secretions of lustful desires in the progression below:

Frame 1: "I will take a drive, but I won't go near that store where pornographic magazines are accessible."

Frame 2: "I will drive by the store but I will not go in."

Frame 3: "I will go in the store because I need to pick up a few items. Yet I will not venture over to the adult magazine rack."

Frame 4: "I will just mosey over to the magazines but avoid looking at any pornography. I'm interested in the articles anyway." (Yeah, right!)

Frame 5: "I will pick up a pornographic magazine, but I will not look at it."

Frame 6: "I will open it, but I will not buy it."

Frame 7: "I will buy it, but I promise this is the last time."

Frame 8: Indulge, indulge, indulge.

Do you see the progression of thought occurring here? We need to daily practice first frame thinking and leave it at that! Don't peer over the edge and see how close you can get to death. Let's take captive every thought and make it obedient to Christ rather than the thought taking us captive (2 Corinthians 10:5). Think and act smart!

ATROPHY OF SPIRITUAL VIBRANCE AND LEADERSHIP: This is the mind-set of "just settling in," or becoming complacent and ineffective in service to family, friends, and God. Over the years I've seen too many men who have given up on being the spiritual leader in their homes and church. They are prone to a "Whatever," "Who cares?" attitude. The damage that can occur when a man is not willing to stand in the gap as a man of God is devastating (Ezekiel 3:17; 22:30).

Have you ever been in an embalming room at a funeral home? It's kind of scary. Bodies lying around are being prepared for friends and family to view. Atrophy of the muscles can quickly set in, causing the body to look contorted if delicate procedures are neglected.

Sometimes our spiritual lives become almost lifeless, giving the indication of atrophy setting in. Overwhelming numbers of men are failing to allow the life-giving blood of Jesus Christ to flow into their lives so that it might affect every area of responsibility and relationship they have.

If our spiritual life is not vibrant, active, and life-giving, then atrophy of the heart and soul is setting in. The result, if we're not resuscitated, is spiritual death. Our family, friends, and church need us more than ever to come alive, and live life to the fullest.

If we can avoid these undercurrents, we will be on track for success at work, home, and with our Lord. But how do we avoid the undercurrents that can so quickly and sometimes unpredictably come into our lives without a moment's notice? How can we avoid getting smashed and swept away by the tug of the world that seeks to pull us under?

What we need is a refresher course on "Basic Life Rescue." Christ seeks to throw us a lifeline and pull us to solid ground, but we must be willing to guard our hearts from the undercurrents that can destroy our lives (Proverbs 4:23). Here are some basic life rescue tactics that need to be implemented in our lives in order for us to become a vessel of honor for the Master's use (2 Timothy 2:21).

REACH: David prayed in Psalm 144:7-8 that the Lord would reach down His hand from on high and deliver him and rescue him from the mighty waters that sought to engulf his life. Take a moment and reach out to Jesus, asking Him to lead you to solid ground. For in Him we live and breathe and have our being, for He is not far from any one of us (Acts 17:27-28). Let's reach out and hold on tight to Jesus before we get pulled under. You will find He's there!

THROW: Are you beaten, bruised, and blemished due to a life of careless living? Then it's time to throw off everything that hinders and the sin that so easily entangles and cast all your anxiety on Him because He cares for you. For it is in doing this that you will find comfort for your aching soul (Psalm 34:18; 63:8; Hebrews 12:1-2; 1 Peter 5:7).

ROW: Have you been rowing into the crosswinds of life? Can you relate to straining at the oars, getting nowhere, and feeling a sense of defeat? Find a trusted brother or sister in Christ who can turn your vessel around so you can find victory over the struggles of life (Proverbs 18:24). Let's stop rowing *away* from those who come to our rescue. Row *toward* them today as they offer godly wisdom for the days to come.

TOW: Are you in need of a tow? In Colossians 1:13, Paul reminds us how Christ has rescued us from the dominion of darkness and brought us into the kingdom of the Son He loves, in whom we have redemption, the forgiveness of sins. Take a moment and ask the Lord to rescue you from those undercurrents you may find yourself in, so that once again you can enjoy the fellowship of His kingdom presence. I know of none other who is so gracious in providing tow after tow for us when we have lost our way.

~ CHARTING YOUR COURSE ~

SELF-EVALUATION

1. What undercurrents are you currently battling? How might they distort your thinking and focus on wholesome living?

2. Are there others that tend to pull and distort your focus on living?

GROUP DISCUSSION

1. How can the undercurrent of pride cause a man to begin resting on his own abilities and personal agenda rather than the guidance of God?

2. Look at Jonah's prayer in chapter 2. What was the cry of his heart when he was swept underneath due to his neglect of the Lord's calling on his life? In what ways can you relate to Jonah on what not to do the next time a strong undercurrent comes your way?

Music Resource: "You'll Get Through This," by Greg Long off of his *Days of Grace CD*, 1995 Shepherd's Fold Music.

Sources
[1] James S. Hewett, *Illustrations Unlimited* (Tyndale Publishers, Wheaton, Illinois, 1988), pp. 433-434.

Navigating
Toward
Valuable Friendships

Chapter 19

A FAITHFUL CREW

Folly delights a man who lacks judgment, but a man of understanding keeps a straight course (Proverbs 15:21).

When a man looks over his life he becomes acutely aware of certain relationships that have been influential in forging character, memories, and growth. The Three Musketeers had each other. It was, "One for all and all for one." The Knights of the Round Table were motivated by the driving passion of, "brother to brother, yours in life and death." The Marines have the honorable Semper Fidelis, "Always faithful," motto, demonstrating the bonds of duty, honor, and country.

There's something about the bonds of friendships that can grip the heart of a man for a lifetime. It is rare these days to find a faithful crew who understand, sympathize, recognize a need, and don't hesitate to confront you with a dose of reality when you've slacked off in the role you play. You are forever grateful when you are blessed with the strength, loyalty, and sacrifice of a faithful crew.

In his book, *When Men Think Private Thoughts*, Gordon McDonald shares about the bonds of intimacy that an ex-marine shared with his platoon in Vietnam.

> I never thought I'd say this, but some of the best days of my life were in the Marines when we were in Vietnam. I ran with a bunch of guys who went through hell together. We saw men

die, get shot to pieces, go crazy. And in the midst of it all we got closer as friends than I ever believed possible. There was nothing we couldn't say to each other, nothing we wouldn't do for one another. You've heard about the guy who throws himself on a grenade to save a friend's life? Any of us would have done that. . . .We talked about everything. We laughed; we cried; we hated; we dreamed; we screamed. . .even had some fist fights. Everything together. But one thing we knew more than almost anything else. *We loved each other in a way that I have never experienced since. I don't think I'll ever have friends like that again* . . . I miss that kind of closeness. The guys I know at church, at work? There's nothing like that with them. Even my wife will never know me like those guys did (italics mine).[1]

One naturally responds in one of three ways after reading this touching example of faithful friendship.

1. *"I don't need that. I can handle my emotions, problems and concerns on my own."* This kind of reaction will leave a man very lonely and hardened to the needs of others around him. This man will isolate himself and will die a death in which few had ever followed his example in life, and even fewer will weep at his passing.

2. *"I am blessed to have experienced that kind of closeness with a few good men over the years."* Responses like this come about because the heart of another has helped a man in the transformation process of his life. His way of thinking and behaving, of showing both toughness and tenderness has been changed because of the influence this friend has had in his life.

3. *"I desire and need a faithful crew of men."* We need men who will support us, pray for us, show tough love to us, rejoice with us, and bleed with us when we are wounded by an attack of the enemy.

It is this third response which we want to address. Plain and simple—solid friendships take time. They can't be rushed, nor can every friendship be molded in exactly the same manner others might prescribe. We can't expect to walk into a new office setting, move into a neighborhood, or go to a dinner party and become best friends with everyone we meet. Like an aged wine, close relationships just can't be rushed.

Proverbs 18:24 tells us that a man who wants friends must show himself to be friendly. Yet, how does the average guy today begin to develop and maintain an ongoing friendship with another man where trust and vulnerability are not feared or seen as awkward? Throughout this book we have alluded to the fact that we need other male friends in our lives who will be a source of strength and encouragement for us as we coordinate our life toward biblical manhood. It is in this chapter that we want to look at four levels of relationship that can be likened to the ones among various members of a ship's crew. The level of relationship determines the type of relationship we can have with the other person. However, we must remember that people grow and change, and so levels of relationship do not always remain static.

CAPTAIN

The captain on any ship has supreme authority. It comes with the task of handling numerous responsibilities. The captain, to the rest of the crew, may only be known by name, title, and face. A crew member living on the lower deck is unlikely to find himself in a close friendship with the captain. It is extremely unlikely that the mate, upon first acquaintance, will find himself sitting next to the captain at the evening's dinner party. His relationship with the captain is as an acquaintance, requiring a mere greeting, a salute, if you will, between them.

Many people we meet are in this category. We make an acquaintance with an individual. The relationship is on the surface level. Nothing more than a few seconds of introduction, a "nice to meet you" gesture and then we move on. Nothing important or of real significance is exchanged. I struggle in even calling these friendships or relationships. In reality they are nothing more than the exchanging of civilities. And yet this is the first level of friendship many of us begin to experience. The fear for many of us is that this is where it ends and our friendships (to use the word loosely) are then based on mere acquaintance rather than anything that might resemble closeness or depth. In order for genuine friendships to occur in a man's life, he must begin to move from the acquaintance or mere introduction level to a more joint interest level.

FIRST MATE

The first mate is directly below the captain in rank. He, too, has responsibility and authority, but his authority stems out more toward the general interest of the crew at large. As we seek to build lasting and significant friendships, many of us will encounter the first mate type friendship.

The first mate friendship could easily be characterized in the following ways.

1. You have a working relationship on the job, but it goes no further than the boundaries of the corporation or job site.

2. It involves small talk (ie., weather, sports, etc.).

3. The bond is usually a common interest. Your sons play on the same soccer team, or you're the only Christians in your workplace. Maybe you're both in the choir.

In other words, your common interests become the focal point of your friendship. In this relationship, we are usually hard pressed to find anything else to say once our arsenal of interests and events have been depleted. For many of us, we are content in leaving our friendships like this. They give us a comfort zone in which we can easily stop talking when we encounter those "I'm not sure what to say now" modes. This level of friendship may be developed over a period of hours or days, but we can't put a time limit on the forging process of genuine friendship. Many of us men have difficulty expressing ourselves on any level. We struggle to make eye contact, ask or even answer pointed questions. Yet by the strength and guidance of the Lord we can move from shallow relationships to the next level of more in-depth ones because of the confidence He gives us to grow with others.

OFFICER OF THE DAY

As a student I remember Mark, the person we called the Resident Assistant, at Moody Bible Institute in Chicago, Illinois. Mark made sure there was order on each floor of the dorms. The only way he could be assured of order was by coming onto the floor. It was through his coming onto our floor on a daily basis that each guy began to see him as someone who was genuinely concerned with the welfare of each student in our dorm.

Over time, closer friendships emerged. We began to open up and share our goals and dreams of what we one day wanted to be and accomplish for the Lord. The day came when we took a risk and began to ask him those below-the-surface questions. I remember his answers were not regimented or rehearsed, but heartfelt. He made us feel like he had all the time in the world to give us and nothing else mattered.

After several months, our relationship grew from the captain and first mate level to a deeper level of appreciation and respect. One night in particular as we were burning the midnight oil studying for exams, he strolled onto our floor with five pizzas from a nearby pizza place. We had jokingly told him all year, "If you want to make friends, you've got to show yourself to be friendly…" and then we would add, "…and that involves bringing pizza." He brought the pizza all right, but he really didn't have to. You see, we had already decided in our hearts that he was welcome on board any time. He was part of the crew.

This level of friendship begins to cut away at the superficial walls we build to protect us from getting hurt or rejected along the way. Instead, it begins to draw on the strength of oneness and on the endless possibilities that true friendship can withstand. Truly, openness breeds openness. Mark showed us that friendship is not something you mechanically produce, but it's something that is forged through spending time being interested and open with one another.

BUNKMATE

It seems from the outside looking in these guys are almost extinct today. Like a rare bald eagle, they are hard to find. But when you reach this level of friendship, you will know it. Don't let these people slip away. This is the Jonathan and David or the Paul and Timothy relationship that we all long for. It takes time and patience. Some of these relationships in my life have developed out of building a more solid friendship in those earlier levels over the years.

If you desire to have a relationship with other men that will fit the above criteria, look at the other ones you have already begun to develop with Christians in your church, in your office, at the gym where you work out, or with a neighbor down the block. Begin to get to know them even better. Step out and take a risk. But instead of trying to make something happen, just let it happen. Simply spending more time with them may do the trick in bringing the relationship to a new level.

I believe there needs to be two warnings here as we seek a soul to soul friendship with another.

1. Be careful about having such high expectations about building lasting friendships that you will be discouraged from trying again when one doesn't work out it. Recently two men in our men's ministry shared that they have known each other for over 30 years. It is just within the last couple of years that they have reached the level in their friendship where they can be open and transparent with each other.

2. Guard yourself from relying too heavily on an individual. Remember that the individual with whom we must have the closest relationship must be our Lord and Savior, Jesus Christ. It is true that our friendships are important. Much of what we do revolves around others, but our friendships should be funneled through the establishment and foundation of an intimate walk with Christ. This must come first if we are to see godly friendships emerge. In other words, godly friendships emerge after establishing a godly walk.

SEVEN "CREW MATE" QUALITIES OF CHRIST-CENTERED FRIENDSHIPS

To find a good friend is to find a good thing. But to find a great friend is to strike gold! Take a moment and evaluate the seven qualities of a great crew mate, and then ask yourself if these qualities are evident in your own life.

ACCEPTANCE—to be fully known, accepted for who you are in Christ, without becoming someone's "project." Look for someone who will accept you not on the basis of your current situation, but will look beyond to what you can fully become in Christ.

UNDERSTANDING—to be listened to without interruptions and to feel "safe" in sharing areas that need to be worked on and victories that can be beneficial for all. Look for a man who will be genuinely interested in helping you to be more like Christ; and who, in turn, would like you to do the same for him.

WILLINGNESS—to be committed to fellowshipping regularly. Someone who will not disappear, but be a man of his word. Someone who is in it for the long haul, and will, with endurance and perseverance, be a conduit toward biblical living.

This past summer I read a fascinating book, *Undaunted Courage*, by Stephen Ambrose. It is a compelling report of the adventurous expeditions of Lewis and Clark. I was struck by the attitude that both of these men had toward their crew who weathered storms, Indian attacks, starvation, and disease to endure this remarkable test of courage journeying from the Ohio River to the Pacific Ocean. Here is an entry from Lewis' diary on the faithfulness of his crew:

> Outstanding leadership made possible the triumph over the Rocky Mountains. We have welded the corps of discovery into a tough, superbly disciplined family. They have built an unquestioning trust in themselves, and know the strengths and skills of their men intimately. Through great hunger and fatigue we as captains have managed to keep morale from collapsing. The men never sulk, lash out, demand retreat, or insist on some alternative route. [2]

These men were not only committed to the mission, but their commitment went deep for one another. Their souls connected in some way through this venture, causing them to endure and persevere. If left by themselves, they may have given up or given in to more convenient alternatives. We need men in our lives who will defend and support, not condemn and discard. Men who will demonstrate a balance between toughness and tenderness. Men who remind us that yesterday's worthlessness can become tomorrow's treasures.

SELF-DISCLOSURE—To risk revealing struggles and shortcomings, without the fear of rejection, criticism, judgment or breach of confidentiality from another. Trust, honesty, a longing to grow, and encouragement by all, need to be prerequisites.

AVAILABILITY—To be available at any time if someone is struggling and needs to talk. True friendship often occurs not when it's convenient for us, but inconvenient. That is the true test of the value of the friendships you are seeking to build. The willingness to put your personal agenda aside in order to come to the rescue of one of your crew members because you want to help shows whether you are truly a friend.

GENUINENESS—For you to always be who and what you say you are. To look into the eyes of another brother in Christ and say, "Hey, brother, I've been there. I know exactly what you're thinking and feeling. How can we help each other and grow together?" Look for someone who helps you focus more on tomorrow's possibilities rather than yesterday's regrets.

CONTENDS FOR THE FAITH—Jude, in verse three writes to fellow believers, compelling them to contend, fight, and defend the faith. We need men surrounding us who are doing just that. They have a vibrant and passionate spirit to thirst after truth, to walk in truth, to remain true. They deal with the issues of the day, but their main quest is to push you closer to the cross of Calvary by helping you to restore self-confidence that has been damaged due to some unwise decisions you made. I have a friend I meet with on a regular basis who fits this quality. Every time we meet, I walk away with a sense of greater passion, purpose and perspective towards living each day for my Lord as if it were my last.

Stu Weber in his book, *Locking Arms*, points out that friends are like highways. They lead somewhere. They take you to a destination. They shape your destiny. And a trusted friend always takes a high road. True friendship never seeks its own. Friendship never acts unbecomingly. Friendship never rejoices in unrighteousness. It always rejoices with the truth. A true friend bears all things, believes all things, hopes all things, endures all things. But friendship never destroys anything. It always builds. It never drags. It contributes to character. It does not dilute it.[3]

I'm sure there are other qualities that can be sought out, but develop these qualities in yourself first, and as like attracts like, you will soon find them in someone else.

BARNACLES - DRY DOCK - OVERHAUL

What do solid and biblical friendships seek to accomplish in an individual's life? I have narrowed the purpose of lasting friendships down to three levels.

BELOW THE SURFACE—Barnacles are pesty little saltwater shell fish that will attach themselves to the underside of a ship. If left unattended, like bacteria, the fish will continue to multiply causing the progress of a vessel to slow down and will eventually result in dry rot. A person may give the indication that his life is "together" on the surface. His talk is right; his disciplines seem polished. But appearances can often be deceiving. Down below the waterline, the darkness of sins often lurks, longing to attach itself and slow him up and eat away at his character. It should be the purpose of a faithful crew of friends to help wash the barnacles of sin from our life by helping us take steps to maintain a tight ship so we can maneuver our life on a steady and efficient course toward holiness (Psalm 51:7-10; 139: 23-24).

ON THE SURFACE—Several years ago I was physically, emotionally, and spiritually exhausted. I was in desperate need of a vacation, but I kept putting it off. I pushed myself, thinking that I would catch up on things and in time things would be just fine. Boy, was I wrong. It was on a Wednesday evening at our men's ministry meeting when I realized I had nothing to give, nothing to offer; I was spent. Emotionally and spiritually I had depleted what I had in my reservoir of passion and drive. I broke down half way through our meeting and shared where I was at with the men. I was overwhelmed as the men began to encourage, affirm and put a sense of worth back into my reservoir. It was one man in particular whose words I will never forget. "Craig," he said, "you are in dire need of 'dry dock.'"

I gave him a strange look and asked in an embarrassed tone, "What's dry dock?"

"Dry dock," he said, "is when a ship which has been used extensively at sea and been exposed to the elements for long periods of time is taken out of the water and place on a dry dock. There it will be tended to, refurbished, and pampered. Any water it has taken in will be pumped out. Any repairs that need to be done will be handled, and any new construction will be added during this time. But the most important element of dry dock is it gives the ship a chance to rest and be restored at the hands of a faithful crew."

Just like a ship, we too need time in dry dock to rest, to be restored, to be refurbished so we can be sent out with stronger passion and purpose for another day. It is a faithful bunkmate who can detect when you have pushed yourself to your limits and who can tell you that you need to step back and be ministered to (Jeremiah 6:16; 30:17; Isaiah 57:15-16,18).

ABOVE THE SURFACE—Dean Merrill, in his book, *The God That Won't Let Go*, shares a vivid picture of how God desires to enlarge our capacity for Him and others through stronger bonds of love.

"A number of years ago I was speaking at a church in Manitowoc, Wisconsin, a port city on Lake Michigan. My host took me that afternoon to see the harbor area. A lake freighter nearly a block long was tied up, and I stared at the gaping hole several feet wide that ran from bow to stern on its side.

"What's happening?" I asked. "Why is there such a huge cut all along the ship?"

"They've brought her in to overhaul her—actually to enlarge her capacity," was the reply. "They have literally sliced the thing right through the middle, jacked up the top half, and now they're welding in pieces to fill the space. When they're done, the ship will carry almost twice as much cargo as before." [4]

I couldn't help but think that men, too, come to Christ ripped apart—by sin and pain. God uses these times, with the help of a faithful crew, to enlarge our capacity to know, serve, and worship Him. Assuring us that He is not finished with us, He shares with us His desire to rebuild our lives, to expand our heart far beyond what we could ever imagine (Psalm 130; Ephesians 3:14-21).

Do you know of a few men who can sail with you on your journey home, keeping your course set towards the mainland? If you don't, there's no better time than right now to climb on board and begin to develop relationships that will perhaps one day become a faithful crew.

Friendship takes time to season into trust. Like water in a deep well, honest expressions of the heart bubble up to the surface rather slowly. A man could go all his life and never taste the cold, bracing refreshment from such a well. But once you've tasted it, the tepid, surface stuff will never satisfy.[5] Stu Weber, author of *Locking Arms*.

Let's lock arms and drink deep from the well together, being refreshed by the words of a caring brother and the comfort of our loving Savior.

If one falls down his friend can help him up. But pity the man who falls and has no one to help him up." Ecclesiastes 4:10

CHARTING YOUR COURSE

SELF-EVALUATION

1. What words or images come to mind when you hear the word friendship?

2. What experiences, good or bad, have you had in stepping into a friendship setting with other men?

3. By reading Proverbs 13:20 & 27:17,19 what benefit will we receive in having a faithful crew?

4. Of the four levels of solid friendship, which one(s) do you need to probe deeper into as you meet with those who desire to see lasting change?

5. Read John 15:12-14. How can the love of God be transferred into your circle of friends when men decide to obey God in their thinking and behavior?

6. Look back at the seven qualities that make up a faithful crew. What qualities do you see in yourself? Are there any men who you know that come to mind who demonstrate these qualities, and might there be an interest in getting together?

GROUP DISCUSSION

1. What are some typical fears and concerns men have about developing closer friendships?

2. What excuses do men use to avoid getting involved with other men who desire to be men of integrity? Are any of these excuses valid?

Video Resources: *A Mandate for Mentoring* with Howard Hendricks— defining moments selected from previous Promise Keepers speakers. Promise Keepers, P.O. Box 103001, Denver Colorado 80250-3001, 1996

The Amazing Precision Marching Band. A humorous drama about an individual who is trying to be a great marching band, but he has no team who is supporting him. Put out by Edge TV, Youth Specialties Edition 23. 1-800-616-EDGE P.O. Box 35005, Colorado Springs, Colorado 80935.

Music Resources - "Pray Me Home" by Phillips, Craig and Dean, off their *Where Strength Begins* CD.

"That's What A Brother Is For" by Michael James off of his *Shoulder to the Wind* CD.

Sources
1. Gordon MacDonald, *When Men Think Private Thoughts*, Nashville, Tennessee: Thomas Nelson Publishers, 1997, pp. 16-17.

2. Stephen Ambrose, *Undaunted Courage*, New York, New York: Simon and Schuster, 1996, pp. 293-294.

3. Stu Weber, *Locking Arms*, Portland, Oregon: Multnomah Books, 1995, p.242.

4. Dean Merrill, *The God Who Won't Let Go*, Grand Rapids, Michigan: Zondervan Publishing House, 1998, p.118.

5. Stu Weber, *Locking Arms*, Portland, Oregon: Multnomah Books, 1995, p. 206.

EPILOGUE
THE MAINLAND

The sun has set, the day is almost finished. A pleasant wind comes from the east filling the sails with life once again. The crest of the moon appears, giving the vessel its only source of light as it cuts its way through the ocean toward home.

It's been a long journey. The days have been long and the nights even longer. A journey where character is forged and loyalty is reborn in the hearts of noble men. A journey where tears have flowed like wine. Where laughter has been shared by those closest, refreshing the soul of man. Where grief and struggle have gripped and torn at a man's dignity.

It's been a hard journey. Days of reminding ourselves of whose we are, and the quest to keep going. Days of engaging the enemy, of contending for the faith, of guarding the heart. Where wounds and scars give evidence of one's allegiance to the Morning Star, the great I AM, the Captain of our soul. Days of searching, hoping, watching for the mainland—a place we call home. Where pain, heartache, and sorrow no longer exist. Where the presence of the One who has formed and fashioned us awaits our coming.

It's been a passionate journey. Where heart, soul, determination, and friendship fuse together in lasting bonds of love. Where passion for our Lord goes deeper than the oceans sailed and kept us stronger than the storms we've faced. Where friends held onto friends when all seemed lost. Where comforting became a necessity rather than an option.

Where talk of what we have and will become is greater than life's regrets and misfortunes. When hope speaks out concerning what we will say to new and familiar faces when our eyes behold our destination.

It's been a growing journey. To thirst after truth, to walk in truth, to remain true. Days when patience was tested and courage defined. Of waiting and trusting that His Word is His bond. Of acknowledging that His promises never fail . . . He is my guide.

I walk to the bow; suddenly my eyes fix on what I have longed for, what I live for—the mainland. The lights, the radiance of this celestial home, the glorious sound of worship and praise now overshadow all my fears, pain, and burdens of the past. For somewhere on the shores of the mainland, stands my Lord, my Father, with open arms waiting to look into my eyes and lovingly say, "My son, welcome home."

Finish Line Ministries was founded in 1992 with the purpose of "Calling the church worldwide to biblical obedience." Finish Line Ministries is an interdenominational revival ministry which travels the country and the world, preaching and teaching the truths of God's Word. The Lord has used this preaching and teaching to change thousands of lives, as individuals have either found salvation in Jesus Christ, or recommitted themselves to a closer walk with the Savior.

Finish Line Ministries provides a wide variety of gifted speakers and resources in helping people establish a strong spiritual foundation with God.

For future bookings and speaking engagements, call or write:
Finish Line Ministries
PO Box 14343
Columbus OH 43214-0343
(614) 538-6077
Email: flm@finishlineministries.org
Website: www.finishlineministries.org

OTHER BOOKS OF INTEREST TO MEN
Available from your local bookstore or call 888-670-7463.

PERSONAL DEVELOPMENT/LEADERSHIP

A Gathering of Eagles by Col. Jimmie Dean Coy
More than 300 Medal of Honor recipients, ex-POWs, and military, political, and religious leaders share their core beliefs about leadership, success, and significance.
ISBN 1-58169-049-5 320pg. PB $14.95

The Power of Forgiveness by Robert Strand
Forgiveness is a dynamic force that can change people's lives. Filled with stories that demonstrate its unique power.   ISBN 1-58169-050-9 96 pg. $5.95

Life Is a Gold Mine by Dr. John Stanko
Thousands of people around the world have been challenged by this book. It teaches the Christian how to effectively and efficiently fulfill their life's mission.
ISBN 0-9637311-2-2 192 pg. PB $11.95

So Many Leaders...So Little Leadership by Dr. John Stanko
A blueprint for leaders from a Christian perspective, this book uses a cutting-edge approach to leadership coupled with biblical servanthood to help leaders become all that God meant them to become.   ISBN 1-58169-048-7 160 pg. PB $9.95

The Face of Anger by Jim Daniels
Shows how to identify the roots, warning signs, and behaviors associated with anger, and gives practical steps to deal with them.   ISBN# 1-56043-247-0 48 pg. 8.5 x 11 Softcover Workbook $6.99

LIFE PURPOSE

Here Am I, Send Me! by Alan Barrington
Learn how to reach your full potential for a more effective personal ministry. Practical help in recognizing God's purpose for your life.   ISBN 1-58169-033-9 192 pg. $11.95

When the Call Seems Small by Clayton Scott
Written to exhort and encourage the person who is endeavoring to fulfill God's purposes regardless of identity, location, or vocation.   ISBN 1-58169-035-5 160 pg. PB $8.95

I Wrote This Book on Purpose by Dr. John Stanko
In a humorous, penetrating style, the author helps you sort through your life and determine what God has in mind for you.   ISBN 1-58169-011-8   128 pg. PB $7.95

DEVOTIONAL

Heaven on the Links by Jim Croft
A devotional for the avid or beginning golfer. Includes golf tips and thoughtful devotions that speak to the heart of men.   ISBN 1-58169-015-0   160 pg. PB $8.95

A Daily Dose of Proverbs by Dr. John Stanko
Here's a devotional that makes Proverbs come alive. With wit, humor, and candor, the author illuminates the wisdom of Proverbs in the context of today's needs.
ISBN# 0-9637311-8-1   376 pg. PB $14.95

BUSINESS/FINANCE

The Little Book of Business Wisdom by Brian Banashak
Business wisdom for the novice and veteran alike. Packed with 88 principles for success—each with Scripture verse and testimony.   ISBN 1-58169-041-X   96 pg. PB $5.95

Money and the Christian by Caleb McAfee
Would you like to earn more, save more and give more? Would you like to enjoy true financial freedom & debt-free living?   ISBN 0-9656010-0-5   192 pg. 8.5" x 11" Softcover $14.95

Proverbs of Success by John Grogan
The heart and soul of highly effective people. The author has shared his wisdom with audiences here and abroad.   ISBN 1-58169-045-2   96 pg. PB $5.95

Start Your Own Business by Caleb McAfee
This practical book has helped countless people fulfill their dream of owning a successful business.   ISBN 0-9656010-1-3   368 pg.   8.5" x 11" Soft. $24.95

HUMOR

Hey Brudder Dan! by Dan Zydiak
Come along with Dan Zydiak, the aspiring writer turned church custodian, who got more than he bargained for when he took the position. Heartwarming and hilarious.
ISBN 1-58169-020-7   96 pg. PB $6.95